IN THE COUNTRY

'In the short term, man seems to have it taped, to have gained dominance over the planet: in the longer term I think we may be the losers . . .

'Because mining operators smartly respond to invitations to dig up quick profits and don't care where. Because central Government—Labour and Tory—flouts the law for a cut in the commercial gain and has encouraged the wrecking of our National Parks. Because local authorities betray the trust vested in them. Because landowners agree to it.

'Money talks. Beauty is voiceless . . .'

In the Country

Kenneth Allsop

CORONET BOOKS
Hodder Paperbacks Ltd., London

First published by Hamish Hamilton Ltd 1972
Coronet edition 1974

Printed in Great Britain
For Coronet Books, Hodder Paperbacks Ltd.,
St. Paul's House, Warwick Lane, London, EC4P 4AH
by Richard Clay (The Chaucer Press), Ltd.,
Bungay, Suffolk.

ISBN 0 340 18637 2

For
Michael Hudson and Brian Jackman
Wessex companions

Introduction

THERE is nothing special, in Britain, about living somewhere which has been lived in for a thousand years—indeed, in a kingdom so close-grained with human occupation it would be difficult not to do so, even in a suburb. Where the sense of continuity comes through with strong vibrations is, of course, if the house itself has been the home of trains of predecessors and has served a consistent purpose. To be included in the long, uncalled roll is a privilege which is both enhancing and humbling: you are merely another entry on that densely-layered palimpsest, and that is sufficient.

I write this near to a steady rush and thunder of water, but I have consciously to listen for it because it flows into the whole composition of the sounds of this small valley, and is euphonic. That is true in another way, too: the muffled roar comes from a river which long ago was pent in a culvert to supplement man's muscles by driving a wheel and, having been diverted to lend this extra power, the chalk stream from the adjacent escarpment is returned, unchanged and as fresh, to its parent race—a good way to work with nature.

A dwelling was first built on this riverside site for that benefit. I don't know when that was, but it is stated in the Exeter Domesday that then, in 1087, the land belonged to the Abbey of St. Peter at Cerne, and that the Abbot's rake-off in geld was from—as well as from four hides (a measure), four ox-teams, demesne lands, villeins, bordars and serfs—a mill (this mill) which contributed 5*s*. 5*d*. The manor in all paid £9 a year, which made it the highest taxed village in the parish. That also sends an empathetic ripple across the centuries.

In a pamphlet concerning the district is this remark about my village: 'After the Middle Ages it seems to have relapsed into a peaceful obscurity, and such records as exist for the period between the fourteenth and eighteenth centuries suggest a self-contained rural parish in all essentials resembling its neighbours'. Self-containment for four hundred years! Isn't that marvellous?

There was a bit of a stir during Cromwell's Protectorate, when the Reverend Henry Brown was sequestered and Henry Hallett, 'an intruder' (a usurper of the ecclesiastical benefice) arrived as replacement. Then, after the Great Fire of London, when St. Paul's Cathedral was being rebuilt (with Portland stone, from the county's own quarries) my village was moved to donate 1*s*. 6*d*. to the fund. Agreed: a moderate degree of involvement.

Otherwise, during that passage of time there was the cycle of the seasons. After Lent, or the Anglo-Saxons' Lengtentide, the sun's trajectory began arching higher across the sky. All hands turned out to scythe and thresh the corn. And my house rumbled with the turn and swash of the wheel, and the grinding of the three round stones, to fill the bins for the darkness ahead when, as the sun curved lower, rural England once again battened down to live out the winter. Now and then a new gaitered cleric would arrive on a tired horse. Hurdlers would be cutting their hazel stands for pinfolds and thatching spars. Geese would be driven along packhorse ways to Emminster market. Some common-fields were enclosed and carved up by three lords of manors to increase their sheep pasture, and peasants who did not take their eviction quietly were briskly put down. In the architectural flowering before the great monastic abbeys' end in the early 1500s two fine halls near here were splendidly reconstructed. Most tenants, the shearsmen and turf-cutters and squatter farmers, probably lived briefly and rheumatically in their mossy-damp cob hovels.

People were, as people always have been and presumably always will be, happy and unhappy.

But four hundred years of obscurity . . . how enviable!

Even after that, despite intrusions of agricultural slump and attempted invasion, despite the attention drawn to this region by the increasing fame of Thomas Hardy's novels (which did not drain from it but thickened its texture), the alterations in the tempo of life and physical surroundings have been slighter than in most places. Although the only German bomb to smite these parts in World War Two fell a hundred yards from where I sit, leaving some fissures in an outbuilding's masonry, it was swallowed up and smothered by the resilient Wessex soil.

I was elsewhere at the time, but I already knew the country, from childhood visits, and eventually I came to settle in it. A writer has an advantage over many other wage-slaves in that, if not quite in a state of manumission, his liege to the system is less intractable: as long as his wits stay productive and his finger joints unarthritic, he can—even allowing for London trips to newspaper office or television studio—organize, or perhaps ad lib, his life more flexibly. He can live almost anywhere.

That advantage, as with most, is not a double-headed coin. There is not for him the same clear distinction between work and leisure. Writing is pretty wholly absorbing; it floods into all hours. The built-in paradox is that, so as to earn the freedom to base himself beyond the commuter belt in surroundings he values, he sees less of them than he does of his typewriter keyboard. Petulantly speculating at the dinner table to my bored family about the worth of keeping them and the establishment going, I on one occasion proposed that we rename the house The Old Mill Stone. Other nominations were put forward: Thruther Mill, The Paper Mill, The Old Treadmill, and so on, and my daughter, who has a sardonic turn of mind, suggested The Dark Satanic Mill. At that time, head of BBC's TV Current Affairs Group, for which I was working, was my old friend John Grist, and I added that I simply had to make sure that he came down so that I could greet him as being Grist to my mill, which seemed to wring the joke dry.

Actually that was not in any sense a serious discussion, for the satisfactions of being fortunate enough to live in what I maintain is beyond contestation the loveliest part of the United Kingdom—the last place left, I think, and the one I love most—put all other considerations out of court. One of those satisfactions was not foreseen.

Not long after moving here I was telling Arthur Brittenden, then editor of the *Daily Mail*, about the buzzards which sail across my garden from their pine-wood eyrie and about the barn owls in the tumbledown lime kiln up the lane, and he said: 'Why don't you write about it all, just as you've been describing it to me—every week?' I began to do so. The unexpected satisfaction was the response that those Saturday morning *In The Country* short articles evoked. In twenty-five years of journalism nothing I had written had drawn such a spontaneous volume of letters, most written direct and personally to me, and it was immensely rewarding to know that so many people who felt cut off from the countryside and its wild life, and were thirsty for it, got from them some replenishment.

There was, incidentally, one correspondent who accused me of delusions of grandeur in appropriating the use of Hardy's fictitious names for real places; I could only reply that it was done in homage—and to preserve a modicum of secrecy. There were many more asking if the pieces would be collected in book form. That, with some amplification and rearrangement, has now been done.

KENNETH ALLSOP

January

And how do the prospects for the coming twelve months look from this side of the realm, beyond the range of high chalk which juts like a midrib down from Wiltshire? Count on me to bring glad tidings of great joy.

Now if New Year's Day were to be falling upon a Thursday it would be altogether a different cauldron of mouldy haddock. Then (I almost dread to mention) we would have to be girding ourselves for: 'Winter and summer windie. A rainie harvest . . . flesh shall be deare; cattel in general shall die; great troubles; warres.'

I have to nerve myself to take an occasional apprehensive peep at my dog-eared Wessex check list of calendar and weather lore for it is distinctly weighted on the side of doom and calamity.

Actually even a Thursday start to January does not mean unremitting blackness. A wet harvest is also guaranteed to bring in train 'much fruit; plentie of honey'. And I would not guarantee that, whatever day of the week, your Sunday hunk of flesh will not continue to be ever more deare.

Yet you perambulate through these ancient records accompanied by spectres of hunger and fear. You can feel the bone-numbing cold of the recluse hamlets and farms when winter sleet tore through the miry coombs of the remote uplands. How bleak and hazardous life was when produce from the strip-lynchets, the common fields scraped out of the switchback slopes and forest brush, had to be eked through the iron months of frost.

In the Merrie England of the early 1880s a boy from these parts was deported to Australia for stealing a pair of boots. An oxen-teamster's wage was nine shillings a week. The Wessex labourer lived on barley bread and potatoes. Caught poaching a deer, he was publicly whipped and put in Casterbridge Gaol. Hardy was haunted all his life by the memory of a child crowstarver being found dead under a hedge—dead of starvation.

Although Hardy, in Irving Howe's phrase, transformed the Wessex landscape into 'a scene of vastness and echo', where a sense of the past lingers 'like a heavy aroma', it was not sentimental nostalgia. There is much to be un-nostalgic about.

Today under the thatch are fridge and deep freeze. Butcher's and dry cleaner's vans scurry down the 'shoots', the tunnel lanes like ski runs. The farm worker and his family take holidays and the boss has a swimming pool behind the Dutch barn. At the school on the steep street of Poorstock mothers turn up in cars to collect their tiny ones—who run out sturdy, aglow and laughing.

The steel rakes on the cottage chimneys scoop from the ether coloured pictures of quiz games, and of distant field workers dying in rice famines and under napalm splashes.

Isolation has, in all senses, diminished. Any decent person must look with thankfulness upon the less arduous life in Britain's countryside. Yet unavoidably he looks, too, upon the supergrid's 164-foot heavy duty pylons, which, to bring light to scattered villages and homesteads, monstrously deface sublime downland.

Only two miles from where the stream gurgles—as if with a cry of joy—from the subterranean galleries into the brightness of sky and open cowlease, I stand on the parapet of the meadow weir watching the synthetic rainbows of detergent wavering down like death rays—

so swift is man to pollute. I see a powerful tractor slashing its ploughshares through prehistoric barrows and earthworks.

Even without those 'warres' and 'great troubles', will the balance of quality and quantity be righted in the time ahead, the little time left to make up our minds if we really want to shift course?

Whichever day of the week—even dodging a Thursday start to the New Year—I would find it hard to be that optimistic.

*

Now is the time of year when up in London friends remark jovially: 'So you got out of it, did you?' I watch their lips shaping the next predictable hackneyed remark. They produce it as if sizzling hot from a newly-forged branding iron: 'Of course the country's very nice in the merry month of May, and all that, but it must be hell in winter.'

I merely stare blankly and cuttingly change the subject. I could (but it is too wearisome) ask sarcastically what's so cosy about sodium lamp land in January.

Why is it better to have rain sluicing through their thin townee shoes? Where's the fun in jousting with every oncomer, umbrellas locked like stags' horns, while exhaust fumes soak from gummed-up traffic into air like soggy blotting paper? What's so super about stepping out of excessive central heating into excessive general colding, just to squeeze into an overcrowded pub at lunchtime?

A pub. Now there's the weakness in my unvoiced argument. That's my furtive problem. The knife again pierced deep as I squelched back to the mill from a walk over our protective redoubts of hills through thickening drizzle. Past, I went, the lightless window from whence once came the pleasant whiff of hops, the murmur of Wessex voices and an iridescent twinkle from the quaint rustic jukebox thundering such folk-song as *Blue Suede Shoes*.

I spend many a contented hour up at the Horseshoes, along the lane in Poorstock. But you can't buy a glass of beer in my village. In days of yore—up to eighteen months ago—there was an inn. The brewery decided to close it. How dare they without taking a referendum?

Those city summer excursionists who feel insecure out of sight of a telephone kiosk, unless all weather forecasters agree about cloudless blue stretching infinitely ahead from the perihelion, are mistaken in supposing that the winter countryside is a dangerous swamp.

I am not sure that this is not my favourite period. It is when the countryside comes clean. It has been scalped of all fussy tresses. Lapwings and fieldfares roughride the winds, golden plover flash like glinting metal filings as they hurl toward the magnet hoop of black nimbostratus pincering around Haggerdown's ridge. A flight of a dozen duck (their wings shine with white patches, like undipped headlights—wigeon) hum along the coast toward the Isle of Slingers.

The trees along my path inland are black X-ray plates of skeletal structure; the hills are gnawn down to the bone by sheep, planes and angles sandpapered by the winds. Ice puts a polish on the cattle close quagmires.

You look at the earth's hard frame and feel it ring on your boot leather. I walk farther and see more across bare, deserted distances. You can see the shape of England, the fanned-out rock sternum from eastern counties joining here under the soft flesh of Wessex.

Because I walk more at this time of year I get thirstier. I felt this keenly as I came past the ruined church tower on its platform of land toward the pub with no beer. I do not demand a gin palace at every corner, merely that it is written into the constitution of the nation that every village must, as a public service and a monument to more sensible civilizations, maintain a pub.

*

This is also the time of year that I go to the seaside. I live only five miles from the sea. Between May and September I deliberately forget it.

If I am winkled out of my valley to go to London, on the return journey I slink off the coast road the moment I can, forking into the furtive lanes and over the great divide of Haggerdown.

Behind me is left the jolly procession of twenty m.p.h cars towing caravans and boats and crammed with children, faces pressed to windows, tense with anticipated happiness and imagining sand between their toes.

I feel that if I get out of their way they will get there quicker.

So out of my immeasurable goodness of heart I hand it all over to the holidaymakers. Sometimes I climb Round Knoll which rises from my paddock. It is a seraphic hill. It is graceful and smooth as a girl's breast. You stand there at five hundred feet upon the very nipple, the sweet green tip, and look through the wind at what seems all of Albion, a surging tract of greenness which bursts through the girdle of the twin mounts of the Pen and Loosden, the dominant points in the county.

Northward in the haze is the relic primeval oak forest of the Chase, where kings hunted deer. Between is a rippling ocean of down and heath and sky. Turn and there is the real ocean, glittering beyond Port Bredy and the fantastic cliff line. The crags are purple clay and sandstone of saffron. The golden pinnacle of the Cap, the Channel's highest bluff, floats in the shimmer like Merlin's castle. Eastward are the rearing precipices which were once the territory of peregrines but whose eyrie is now a target for tank-mounted rocket-launchers.

At evening herring gulls glide high over the Knoll and their faint yelps arouse a desire to head into the shining mirage of sea and cliff. But I think, no, I don't really want a hot dog or to tour the bay discotheques, so I'll wait.

Yesterday was dull and cold as slate. I went over to Punnel. The shingle curves in a long eight-mile hook which traps a reedy lagoon. A band of silver-winking waders—they were dunlin—zigzagged along the strand. Two magpies flounced over a shuttered bungalow and an empty car park.

Goldfinches fed on weeds beside the padlocked ice cream hut. On the skyline was a tanker, looking for a pleasant place to vomit some oil (four hundred glued-up, dying razorbills and guillemots strewed this beach after a recent slick) but so far that cormorant was fishing in safety.

The row of chalets seemed to have been evacuated in an invasion alarm. The bottleneck lane was a hundred years ago the main ingress point for smuggled cognac and coffee berries off Cherbourg ships, bustled on packhorses for sale in Bath.

This was no piddling operation. In the late eighteenth century the business was run by a Godfather figure named Isaac Gulliver, who ran a Wessex Family of pistol-packing horse-mounted mobsters. He fitted farm-houses and town houses as staging points with hidden chambers in roofs and walls for caching his tea-sacks and kegs of spirits. He even bought a plot on the seaward rump of Haggerdown and planted a marker of trees to orientate his fleets. A resourceful gangster, Gulliver: he once escaped a custom officers' raid by chalking his face and posing as a corpse—and eventually escaped into settled respectability at Warborne, his daughter married off to a banker.

Looking at the track, with its barbican of bramble, it seemed to me that such trade could still be going on. It would never be noticed. Cold waves hissed and splattered on the pebbles, and there wasn't a single delighted squeal from a single toddler. Could there ever have been crowds here?

Above the tideline a carrion crow tugged at some unspeakable washed-up tid-bit. A yellowed pamphlet fluttered under a bent beer can. 'Holiday Bungalets and Camp Site', it said. 'TV Lounge, Corvette Fires, Flush Toilets, Razor Points'.

So it was true. The crow sloped off with a phlegmy snarl, but he didn't bother to go far. He, too, knew when the coast was clear.

*

I was working into the small hours. If words are flowing —or, anyway, dripping—I often do this.

Writing is a peculiar trade, rather melancholy and intensely solitary. There is excitement in picking out a trail across the keyboard, to where you can't always be certain; simultaneously comes the dread of rolling in a blank sheet, the uncharted empty plain to be covered.

At one, two, three in the morning there is a great belljar of silence upon the house and the country around. The lamp's pool of light is your circumference of life, the theatre-in-the-round of your imagination. In Ted Hughes's marvellous poem the fox prowling in the snow outside his window becomes one with his creative process treading tentatively across the white foolscap.

> *. . . with a sudden sharp hot stink of fox*
> *It enters the dark hole of the head.*
> *The window is starless still; the clock ticks,*
> *The page is printed.*

The dense night quiet was broken only by my jerky click-click-click as I built up an image—then, dissatisfied, stengunned it down with a burst of x's.

Another sound obtruded. From the hillside came a nasal yap-yap-yap, as staccato as my typewriter. For a moment I was confused. Which was real? The dog fox barked again, louder, probably swinging his head.

They are mating now. It got a response from farther up my top field. It wasn't exactly a coo-ee. A vixen's amorous cry sounds like the last strangulated screech of a victim garotted by thugs. I was glad that they were getting on so well.

The immense mattresses of bramble up there are citadels of rabbits, which have changed their habits since myxamatosis almost exterminated them. The rabbit is now much less of a troglodyte. The hardier survivors avoid the old burrows where the virus loiters and have adapted to a guerilla life in the undergrowth. Foxes squat outside the spiky caves and wait for a mouthful.

I left my desk and went outside. No mellow yellow. The moonlight was cold, sharp, metallic: the hard shine of durilium. The corn barn was bone-white, its windows black sockets: its fustian shadow was like the hood thrown back from a death's-head.

The weathercock high on its rod gleamed pale gold, a myth in mid air. The sky was so chemical clear that I saw a real night bird, a tawny owl, wafting over the corkscrew chimney on wings dark as dead oak leaves but soundless as snow.

I climbed the wooden steps to the footbridge across the leat. Below, at ground level, you hear the weirfall only as wispy oboe music; on top, the broad front of water crashing down twenty-five feet of spillway has the deafening bass roar of an orchestra of tubas.

In this strange icy moonlight the turbulence down the ten stone steps of the fish ladder looked like billows of steam. Just a few yards on, where it twists out of sight into the ravine under umbrellas of nut-bushes, the water is calm as milk.

That's where the foxes come over. They swim well and casually, so a moat won't stop them. They trot into the garden and sniff under the lime where the guineafowl roost and around the stable housing the two young peafowl.

Descending the steps, I heard the triple-yap again, but this time unanswered. Had the vixen gone off with another? Well, the fox had some dark hours left in which to round her up or jump a rabbit or two; I, a trespasser from daylight, went to earth.

*

From a walk across the water meadows I brought back a few trophies. A spray of alder catkins or a precocious primrose? No. I lurched back like a rural Steptoe laden with rags and old iron.

I hadn't intended to stock up for an oddments stall. I had taken the footpath which cuts across to the village. After April you cannot believe that the mill, in its dead-end hollow and diked around by the forking river, is within carrier pigeon reach of other human habitation.

Now that the trees are stripped, the outlying cottages can be seen from my gate. The lane makes a half-mile loop but on a diagonal line the cardinal's hat spire of the Victorian church peers through the willow grove.

Actually I was not on my way to church. I was going to meditate beside the overfall weir. I keep the weir under surveillance. That helter-skelter of cataracts looks capable of leaping in any direction. I like to be sure that it is in good humour and not showing signs of waywardness.

It is a thirty-feet-wide junction of crestwalls of different levels. The main flow foams down seven steep ledges. Storm-water builds up and topples over the highest rim and there is a frenzy of miniature Niagaras.

There has been a weir here for centuries. Fragments of older bulwarks are smothered in moss and ferns. Ownership of a mill gives you riparian rights but also imposes riparian obligations.

Although this isn't my field, at this point the first millwright built a dam and siphoned off a run. Under curtains of ivy are massive oak sluice panels which control my flow. There begins the long tranquil parabola of the leat which eventually passes through the innards of my house. It has to be kept dredged and soundly banked.

I heard the local story (after having bought the place) of a great flood of twenty years back when, in a freak spring spate, our tame little brook rose maniacally out of its channel and a wall of water raged across the fields, into our declivity and straight through the house, carrying out on the farther side an old lady riding a grand piano like a surf board. Doubtless it is just a fable—but it hangs around in the back of my mind. Indeed, on more than one occasion, when winter gales have been chucking buckets of water at the bedroom window, I have risen and, looking in sou'wester like an heroic lifeboatman in a Victorian steel engraving, wrestled in the drenching blackness with the iron winding handles on the draw-doors of my little control point, to rack up the wickets and divert the rush away from the mill room.

Now my attention was diverted from these grave concerns of watching over the safety of Wessex. The weir looked fine. The decorations didn't. Three empty fertilizer bags of elephant's-hide plastic were draped in the sallows where long-tailed tits were feeding. One was half sunk in the shoals, busy poisoning newts and water snails and frogs with the residual chemical granules from the seed-dressing. I reached down and dragged the sacks out. More was revealed.

I took out an oil can, dribbling contamination. Half submerged was a wheel. From what? It was chunky enough to support a tank, but with effeminate little spokes and knobbly rims. Perhaps it was the first wheel.

The holey frying pan had long since sizzled its last rasher but it was made of immense iron plating, apparently hammered when molten by a squad of smiths. Finally emerged a pink tin inscribed 'Devon Violets Perfumed Talc—Lasting Freshness'.

What an interesting cache. I imagined the burly yeoman who had wobbled across the tussocks on his single wheel balancing three sacks of fertilizer upon his shoulder. Pausing to slake his understandable thirst, over a twig fire he had fricasseed himself a couple of hares in the pan. Replete, he had then languorously dusted himself from forehead to toes with Devon Violets Perfumed Talc.

Possibly then realizing that his life was a hopeless mess and getting him nowhere, he had burst into tears and drowned himself.

I wished, as I struggled with my load to my distant dustbins, that he had set an example to all dumpers by, instead, digging a pit and then scooping earth over his possessions and himself.

*

Up to the day before the snow swept in we were having a little bonus spring down here, a sort of private theatre-club showing. The halcyon sunny mornings were polka-dotted with daisies. The thick overgrown withy-beds of willows flared with scarlet buds, like the sparks of a fire stirring to life and flying upward in the light wind. The shimmer seeped into paler and stronger shades, the pink and purple from the breaking catkins of aspen and alder.

The lime on the back lawn barely got rid of last year's foliage in time to make room for the tips of the new. A mistle thrush was bellowing from an elm top, as if bursting to be nesting. The grass was still growing: enough to be worth turning out the Friesians on to the hills for their meal, an unexpected boost to their milk flush from the precocious sweet tips of lucerne and vetch. The rosettes of spear thistle and ribwort plantain looked to be flourishing on my lawn, I noticed without pleasure.

I was working my way with a sickle along the bank of the pond (cripplingly back-aching but good for muscle-tone, I consoled myself) and hacking away through matted dead cow parsley and nettles.

There on the shrivelled stem of last summer were a ragged robin's new gaudy petals. It was breaking the botanical rules. It should have packed up and stopped flowering in August.

The blizzard put paid to that ragged robin and all the other foolhardy upstarts. Within hours the landscape looked blighted, all that untimely frivolity bashed down by the weather which fell like a steel hammer.

It was too late, though, to put a brake on the pigeons. Months ago I built a loft in the stone barn, cut half-moon holes in the gable clapboard, and erected perches on some curly Victorian cast-iron brackets dug out of a local junk yard. The dovecote's founder members came from a local colony. In October I was sent a cock and two young hens, elegant of line and with the shine of alabaster. I stapled wire netting over the front, and put in corn and water and grit through the hatch inside the barn. They could just take their time acclimatizing themselves and relaxedly settling in until they were allowed to fly free in the spring, I thought.

I underestimated these Wessex pigeons' hormones. The cock was instantly behaving very cockily, pugnaciously puffed up and charging after the scuttering hens, growling with lust and aggression—not looking in the least like an anti-war symbol.

Of course pigeons are birds of all seasons, despite the female possessing only a left ovary. But could they really be mating at this time of low ebb? It did seem somewhat prompt for the adrenalin and estrogen to be flowing so potently. The hens seemed to be retaining some misgivings that it was the wrong time and the wrong place, but the cock looked to be an unflagging all-rounder.

Speculatively I threw in some straw and twigs. They were whisked into a nesting box. By early December the first egg was laid. Clearly they didn't need to be persuaded to stay. I propped up a ladder against the eaves, yanked out the staples and lifted away the wire netting—and one of the hens almost took off my right ear. She shot from the coop and away, a pearly streak across the piebald backs of the grazing herd.

The cock and his faithful wife fluttered out reluctantly. They thwacked clumsily with flabby muscles, then gained confidence. They wheeled wing-to-wing, tightly in unison as two Red Arrow Gnats. They ringed in widening spirals toward the heatless sun shining upon a sugar-icing world. They soared higher, white ripples in a lake of palest beryl-blue, exulting in their airy freedom—but taking bearings of their new home.

A prowling carrion crow cast a glance at the brilliant newcomers and gave a grunt of interest. They levelled off then, having got the measure of their centre, came in a long fast swoop down on to the house roof. A few minutes later the cock was feeding on the gravel forecourt and the hen was back warming her eggs.

The two young, a touch bedraggled with greyish down, made their exploratory stumbling flap into the big outdoors the morning after the first heavy snowfall. As I write they are sitting on the barn between the parent birds, looking out upon a world as bleached as they are, winter misfits with a green future.

*

It has been pointed out that the suspect most likely to be overlooked in a murder mystery is the postman, because no one actually notices him calling. He—like the dustman, the butcher and the newsagent—should be. In the deep country they do doughty service.

Admittedly they are now petrol-propelled. Can you remember when the GPO came by bicycle, sack on back? Until recently we were probably the only diocese in England with a Mountie vicar. Accoutred in clerical collar and jodphurs, he did his parish rounds on a fine chestnut stallion. And what better way of visiting his flock in their sporadic hamlets, divided by our miniature mountains where the worn soil seems stretched so tight that elbows of rock stick out through the frayed rags of turf, and linked often by only spindly lanes which scrape both sides of a car. I can see that it must be less trouble than a horse, and certainly has more horsepower, but I do personally regret that the vicar has now gone over to a zippy MGB.

Our daily callers all go to great lengths, and great distances, to perform their duties—the postman in particular. In its twice-daily delivery to the mill the red Morris Minor has to skewer down those fosse-like lanes, gooey with mud from cows' hooves, negotiate half a mile of thorn-ambushed track to a large iron gate (which must be opened and shut as a nominal gesture against mass breakouts of animals) and then twist and turn around sheds and barns to the delivery box.

When the bundle consists of bills, a Special Offer of *The Magic Carpet Encyclopaedia of Universal Knowledge* for twenty pence a week spread over sixty-five years, an invitation to open a bazaar in Bannockshire, and three letters complaining of the inflexion in my voice when on television uttering a word like 'politician', I suffer aching remorse for the postman's long rural ride.

I try to compensate by lightening the dustmen's toil. What will rot goes into the compost silos, and delights the crows and magpies and rats which lurk around that gamey pie dish. What will burn I heave along to the incinerator, a shaky home-made structure with a lanky brick chimney.

On the last trip with bin of paper on shoulder and a Covent Garden porter's pile of cardboard boxes, the fire wouldn't take. Raking out soddened sandwiches of paper, my eye was arrested by a fragment from a local weekly. There is always much exciting reading in the county papers. This bit was about a court case involving three young men who had drunk eleven pints apiece, and it had an incredible plot.

Two of the cast were named Shoe (but, explained the blurred print, were not related although living in the same village) and the other's name was Boot. Boot 'was cut'. One of the Shoes asked Boot who kicked him. Boot said he had not been kicked. The other Shoe then said to Boot: 'If you don't tell us who kicked you, we'll kick you.' They then proceeded to kick each other in a mêlée of shoes and boots—and there the print fizzled out in a charred frill.

How maddening. In the sleety drizzle, which was washing away the snow, I poked away at the smouldering heap. Would I—as in a spy novel—find the missing piece of this melodramatic jigsaw?

A robin, hopeful that I was turning over insect-rich clods, flitted across, eye cocked. It seemed that we were both unlucky. No other clue surfaced. I didn't know which paper it came from or how old it was, so I would never find out what happened to all that turbulent footwear.

All the mystery yielded was some shallow philosophizing that there will in life always be the Boots who get kicked for not already having been kicked.

Then, would you believe it, my iron bar turned up a minute wisp bearing the words: '. . . the Shoe boys then took Boot to hospital. . . .'

What an ending! Not up to some films and fiction for bucolic violence, perhaps, but I hope they finished up with arms round shoulders in the out-patients' department, singing harmoniously through bloody lips.

You can see what important emissaries are the men who drive through hail and high water to keep us abreast with the events of the outside world.

February

THEY were out, pushy as ever, when there was hardly any daylight worth speaking of. Fearful show-offs. On the dankest coffin-like days of deep winter, the snowdrops were already flaunting themselves among the mushy shells of last autumn's apples.

Of course it was a treat to see them, lamps through the year's overcast. Yet I know that I'm being led up the garden—quite literally—when I espy these first scraps shivering in the wind. It's hard to credit that a flower so chastely white can be so dyed in deceit.

For that fanfare to spring blown by those small trumpets is a false note. After their blooming is over can come the nastiest weather, the gales which rip away the tassels from the hazels across the stream and quench the ruddiness of the birch catkins.

But how can the snowdrops be dismissed? I had taken the path beside the untended old plums, the once regimented, diagonally-pruned Kirk's Blues and Victorias and Transparent Gages, now knottily run riot. The soddened rank grass had stiffened with frost, the sky was cement cold, the hedge looked lifeless as rusted wire—how could tender buds thrust through that black iron? The sycamore trunks were coated with a silvery fungus which had crisped like meringue with the fall in temperature.

The snowdrops reminded me of the forces under the

ice-enamelled earth, the insistence of the life-renewing cycle—a billion miniature sunrises. The reds and blues don't daub the hedge-banks and grassland until the sun has got up on to its high summer rostrum and is applying strong brush strokes. At the start of the year the colours are blanched: whites and wan yellows.

This little hoaxer is tough behind its air of frailness. The corolla so flexibly swivels on the stalk that no gale will snap it. Moisture slides off the drooping heads, so protecting the pollen. The dazzling whiteness lures whatever rays the sun can generate and the petals clench at night to hug the ember of warmth.

I am lucky. Close by in a shady damp copse is one of the only two native British sites of the bigger spring snowflake, with a fragrance as powerfully sweet in the moonlight, so it is a twenty-four hours food store for both butterflies and moths. But the familiar snowdrop means more. Misleadingly impetuous though it is, it does turn up to do its silvery dance over the sullen clods just when winter is becoming an ache in the joints.

It is believed that it came over with 15th-century monks. It clusters thickly in old monastery gardens. Why? Because—hadn't you noticed?—it was Candlemas Day this week. It was planted to decorate the Feast of the Purification of the Virgin. So it's still, here and there, called also the candlemas bell.

I can't claim, though, that the second of February has always been one of hallowed piety in Wessex. We always, don't we, contrive to get the best of both worlds.

The custom round about, once the window shutters were barred, was to light a monster candle. Until it guttered out the hours were licensed not just for prayer but for swigging ale and punch. The vases of snowdrops, it's my guess, were just a thin sanctimonious screen of purity.

*

I always feel a pleasant throb of surprise—and relief—when I spot a train hoving toward my local station. 'Well, I never—found it again!' I remark to myself incredulously as it slows at the far from thronged platform.

How did this single-track spur line escape Beeching's chopper? My guess is that no one remembered to tell his hatchet squads about it. So a traditionalist engine driver faithfully follows the instructions of some mildewed schedule. A touch surreptitiously, he sneaks along the whiskery sleepers winding around the inland cliffs.

The first narrow-gauge steam service chugged into the county (about twenty-five years later than anywhere else) on a route known as the Corkscrew. What's left of it still twists through countryside not much altered from 120 years ago.

This must be the forlornest station. The nearest hamlet is almost a mile off. The lane goes no further.

Did news of nationalization ever get through? Beyond the causeway an iron notice, bolted to a sagging post, says: 'Rights of Way Act 1932. The Great Western Railway Company hereby give notice that this way is not dedicated to the Public.' How nicely they said keep out in those days.

The ticket office long ago shut up shop—you pay on board. But the office appears to be not entirely unfrequented, perhaps after the midnight flyer. There are hearts containing arrows carved upon the walls, and lists of girls' names which may have some local significance.

A rose has squeezed through the waiting room's warped casement and writhes inside. Yet it must once have been a house-proud halt, for under ground elder are flower beds run wild. Where grass and bird-sown brambles are crumbling the flags is a smothered ornamental pool in a rockery gone ape.

For me the station is a decompression chamber, through which I transfer from the metropolis to the far-flung West and back, in easy stages. Out of how many trains do you step down on to stone dabbed with moss and lichen?

The other morning I stood beside the only poster (advertising the Royal Smithfield Show at Earls Court, December 7–11) waiting for the connecting train up from the coastal terminus.

A magpie waggled away up toward the Hornby-size road bridge and then a jay took exactly the same route—this is a flyway as well as a railway. There was nothing to be heard but sheep calling their lambs and a linnet's twanging guitar-like runs. Cattle browsed among the flowering gorse on the opposite slope, and catkins shivered in a cutting wind which numbed the sunshine.

Looming full ahead, cloud-high, was the gaunt arch of Haggerdown, the earthworks and tumuli underscoring the site of the Iron Age hill fort and where there was the small scale Stonehenge of tribes almost without trace. Even their megaliths are scattered and blanketed under the bracken, sweetbriar and the brushy grass thickets of upright-brome.

The Industrial Revolution reached out an exploratory steel claw into this region. It rusts and flakes away, and anyway is booked for eventual closure. Meanwhile nature is doing the Government's job for it. The countryside will soon have covered the temporary scratch, and I shall have to travel from a busier, mainline place.

*

Indoor plants honestly do defeat me. I never can remember which like to pretend that they are still in the Sahara and those which prefer to squat in a permanent puddle.

I always water the wrong ones. With amazing versatility one will rot damply with canker while its neighbour's leaves wither away to cornflakes with dryness. They all die.

They stand on shelves and shingle-lined trays in a peculiar little annex jutting out beside the gristmill. It's called the flower room, though hardly ever does a bloom give a smitch of colour to that rather glum tangle of plectranithus and tetrastigma and monstera, which have the sound of extinct primaeval lizards of the Mato Grosso. Most are extinct in my midget Mato Grosso.

Therefore when I went in with brimming plastic watering can the other evening I was delighted to see a pulse of active life.

Low in the corner is a brass tap. It trickles screamingly cold water from the hillside into a worn stone sink, which has a simple overflow hole. A round pipe sticks out over the river bank.

As I entered my eye was caught by a twitching movement. I had a glimpse of an immaculate white cravat and sandy fur, and ears big as columbine bells, then there was the tip of a tail whisking away into the overflow pipe.

Doubtless the field mice have discovered the sack of fish pellets which are tossed to the trout in the lower leat. What a winter prize packet to come across! I don't in the least begrudge the success of such enterprise. I am happy that the homestead is shared not just by the spotted flycatchers and pied wagtails which build in the creepers outside the flower room, but by more adventurous lodgers.

When I was originally putting the place in order I rehung the stable door which had gaped askew for years. Sadly, the swallows whose mud saucers were cemented on the beams inside didn't take to the tidying up. They balked at the half-moon holes I cut in the planking, and nested there no more.

Still a pair of wrens recognized a desirable property when they saw one. They used the crescentic hatchway and raised a family in a feather-lined dome of moss on the inner lintel. Robins, house sparrows and chaffinches have been sharp to note that, by sidling through a window left open a notch, there is always a bowl of grain available in the peafowls' pen.

Sometimes a kingfisher perches on the footbridge rail six feet from the window—there seems suddenly, with those prisms of cobalt blue and russet, to be a pane of stained glass. We even have young dippers wandering indoors from their cradle of moss and dead leaves in the stonework of the yew walk bridge. Who would not be gladdened by such callers?

Yet my open house policy shrivelled to nought when I switched on the kitchen light to see, heading for the dogs' biscuits, something rippling across the quarry tiles with a flowing motion of a single elongated foot. Undeniably an exquisite functional article of natural engineering. But I could not warm to that black slug of so many meaty inches. Hospitality withdrawn. So was the slug.

*

I dare say that, just as nothing can be blacker than black or deader than dead, water has no gradations. Water is wet, and by its nature cannot be wettish or furiously wet.

All the same, I swear that the rain which hurls into these West Country clefts, where villages and farms huddle under long greensand ridges, is wetter than any.

When clouds clot like great purple bruises where the Knoll drives its fist at the sky the downpour comes drenchingly thick. Its wetfulness is terrific.

I started scooping out an emulsion of mud, leaves and twigs which was blocking the leat's flow under the lane bridge. Not a drop struck the surface of the river. Yet I was soon soaked: aerosol rain, softly saturating.

I had probably merged with such perfect camouflage into the soddened greyness that the tree-creeper didn't notice me. It lit on the ash leaning over the stream and began ascending the sheer overhang in effortless scuttles. It is not a bird much seen in our thinly-timbered hill country. I watched with interest.

Buff mottled back, silver-white underparts. I could see how it darted up that steep precipice: clownishly big splayed feet grappled on the rough bark, stiff rufous tail feathers worked like a pivot. Slender sickle bill probed into crevices for earwig or woodlouse.

That may not be your sort of tuck. So perhaps you are unenvious of the tree-creeper's specialized equipment for getting at the grub it likes—unreachable by the beaks (too short or too broad) of the long-tailed tits and nuthatches which work over the same tree, but for different food.

That's why a garden supports such a teeming variety of birds. Nature cannot abide a vacuum. With an exactitude far more intricate and discriminating than our wonder dating-service computers (and less likely to commit a blunder equivalent to pairing a tall vegetarian girl with a pork-pie-manufacturer of restricted growth) every niche is filled.

How many blackbirds breed around these rough-and-tumble grounds? The governing factor must be the square yards of open grass. There must be the further mysterious control of not the number of worms now in those turf allotments, but how wormy they will be when each nest holds ravenous babies.

One patient ornithologist carried out an output-input survey on a pair of dunnocks with a brood in his garden. A parent bird visited the young once every five minutes with an average beakload of six grubs. That was a rate of seventy grubs an hour for sixteen feeding hours. So just this one pair of small birds—and not reckoning in their own big appetite to keep them stoked up with energy during that period of terrific activity—were eliminating 1,150 insects, probably mostly pests to the gardener, each day. That's a sum worth bearing in mind when irritated by bird damage to the green peas and apple buds.

We talk of the incessant savage struggle in the wild. In fact competition has, by a subtle social pact yet successfully to be achieved by man, been discarded as wasteful.

The insect-eating robin dwells harmoniously alongside the song thrush which cracks open snails. Even the chaffinch and hawfinch don't war over the same seed supply. Whereas the first's cup runneth over from weeds and flowers, the hawfinch's massive vice of horn can crack nuts which defeat other beaks.

How was my tree-creeper doing? It wavered off through the rain—certainly into other birds' territory, but steering along a fine guide-line of balance leading it only to what it needed, the rest left for others. That seems a good code for living in our world of non-returnable containers, non-consumable rubbish—and non-renewable resources.

*

Here they come again, zipping like rubber bullets across the hedge and straight on to target. They hit the ground like those puffs of dust when Tombstone's main street was being paved with hot lead.

My hail of missiles are feathered. When I first lived at the mill there were, oddly, no house sparrows. Now it is on the calling list of at least forty.

They bring with them handsome burly little birds, whose olive plumage is slashed with bright yellow chevrons: greenfinches. There are usually a few chaffinches, pink as shy girls, jittering about on the edge of the gang. Even the blackbirds—including a spotty part-albino which gives him the look of a dwarf magpie—have tumbled to it.

I am dismissing from my mind the degenerate jealousy and greed of the beagle and the dachshunds. They so carp at any other stomachs sharing the household pot that they charge barking into flying feathers—then stand morosely nibbling at the stuff. They don't even like it. It lodges between their teeth like raspberry pips. But—dogs in the manger—they stubbornly crunch away.

My feelings about the birds are as mixed as the grain they stuff themselves with. Individually I like every last one. Collectively, and locustively, as they home in on the gravel forecourt, they arouse in me a resentful impulse to violence.

They do not just hop about, pecking a seed here, a seed there. They *sit down*. Reclining, they shovel up my grain like mechanical earthshifters. It is the way they settle down so comfortably at their gluttony which puts my teeth on edge.

What is impossible to get across to these winter pirate hordes is that the heaps of kibbled maise and corn are not for them. Nor are they largesse for the other free-loaders who drop by daily for an easy tuck-in, the doves from a nearby farm. The galling part is to see my own four renegades among them.

Recently I was crowing about the white fantails settled in their new cote, how in December's depths they had reared two squabs. I must eat what I suppose is humble pigeon pie.

What happened to the founder members of my new dynasty of doves? No sooner were the two young strong on the wing than they were hived off by their treacherous parents to the clan across the hill.

Having deserted their birthplace, they now bring their new cronies over for a hand-out lunch. I have a searing feeling of being used.

Each day I morosely toss out corn in the stable yard with the pathetically diminishing hope that it will bribe them back to the old homestead. 'Come back to the buildings', is in that broadcasting gesture; 'all is forgiven'.

Each day the sparrows and finches rollick in, bills agape. But soon they will be pairing off and taking up spring territory, and those mass raids will cease.

Each day the pigeons descend, and condescend, to

eat with me—then lumber off with indigestion and never a backward glance. Will it go on thus forever? Why should I be spurned? How can I win them back?

*

I missed the recent nasty weather. It so happened that I had an urgent assignment in the South Pacific.

I can understand now what John Wayne went through, slugging the Nips out of Guadalcanal . . . The terrible glare of all that white sand and iridescent ocean; hobbling over sharp coral to swim; the grave danger of being concussed by a falling coconut.

Back home I found my wife, hearing slightly impaired by the cold virus she had carelessly picked up, curiously inattentive as I told her about this tropical hell. Perhaps it was the rheumatic twinges which made her snappy when I was explaining that it was so hot the hibiscus shrivelled.

It is hurtful to be suspected of false pretences for preferring elms to palms, and partridges to parrots. The morning was murky when I got back on to home ground. The sun above Haggerdown had a look of haggard determination, the face of a patient in a bad way propped on a green pillow to take a sip of nourishment from that bowl of gruel which was the mist clotting the bottom.

On the way through Uploopers the astonishingly ugly Muscovy ducks, with wrinkles and warts like grog blossom on their faces, were waddling and lounging around in the tyre tread marks, and I indulgently nudged them out of the way. I looked fondly down upon the saddleback porkers rooting about in their valley slum, a crater of mud and dung.

I turned down my lane and snowdrops along the stream were the only flecks of brilliance in a suffusion of duns and blacks and greys and dull greens. The hills, hung with mousy plaits of hedgerow and with a ribbon of water at the end looked as plain as a schoolgirl after those gaudy places flaunting themselves like Hawaiian dancers.

My theory is that most scenery has been built by set designers or dictated by novelists. Those seedy South Seas islands, with their white clapboard bungalows clunking with iron fans, have obviously modelled themselves on Somerset Maugham's stories.

I once lived in piney Buckinghamshire, clearly laid out as a location for early Rank B-pictures—those which opened with a long shot of an Armstrong-Siddeley arriving (sound track of crunching gravel and May bird-song) at a Mystery Manor (1930s banker's Plantagenet with stainless steel mullions).

To return from brochure exotica to my Wessex village was like picking up an unfinished Victorian novel, dense and melancholy. Of course these shrouded chalk downs and dells choked with fern were put there on contract for Hardy.

Dropping my bags I renewed acquaintance with the vale where, I don't doubt, Jude gazed yearningly towards Christminster's spires. I walked through my garden and up the slope with its mane of old beeches which must be where Gabriel Oak first saw Bathsheba Everdene.

It was interesting eating paw-paw for breakfast beside a Rent-A-Canoe lagoon, expecting the waiter to break into a Rogers and Hammerstein lyric. But I like best having a bit part in this English story.

*

I eventually decided that I had just better be brazen about the swimming pool. Since living at the mill I have been shifty and embarrassed about it.

'What's over there?' ask friends when they walk out of the sitting room on to the flagged terrace and glimpse under the lime's drooping boughs a white marble head.

'Let's climb up the Knoll,' I say evasively, jockeying them round to the opposite compass point, 'the view from there's amazing.'

Pulling free of my hand steering their elbow, they stride over to the arch beside the juniper, stand motionless for a second, swivel and say in a hostile accusing voice 'A *swimming pool*!'

It is like dropping a Playboy Club membership card and, as you stoop to pick it up, accidentally exposing the mink lining in your raincoat. It is like being trapped into confessing that you sent your children to Eton instead of Holland Park Comprehensive.

None of the above applies to me. But I do have this swimming pool. I almost hadn't. When we made our first exploratory sorties into Wessex to look at houses I tossed aside the particulars of the mill. 'Swimming pool, it says, that's out.'

I could see it. Kidney-shaped fibreglass of stabbing blue, a setting for starlets. Beside the mill-pond would be a *cabana* and barbecue-pit. The house was bound to have a ship's cabin bar.

On that day, nose turned toward the London motorway, barren of possibilities, having looked at ferro-concrete farms and small manors nestling under the steel scaffolding of advance warning radar dishes overlooked by agents, I sullenly diverted at my wife's insistence to look at the crossed-off mill.

It seemed as perfect as anything I could imagine. We bought it not because of the swimming pool, but that is beautiful too. Broad yew hedges surround it. Lawn runs up to the stone coping.

An old catalpa tree towers behind the statue on its plinth, and at her feet bubbles the spring from the hillside. It is tranquil and formal as a Roman bath.

It is also paralysingly cold, that dribble which serpentines through a spaghetti bowl of underground piping. When we first saw it the water was tea-coloured with decayed leaves and fur-trimmed with algae.

We turned off the cock and drained out 21,500 gallons. On broiling summer days my sons slaved down in the chamber, hacking away with metal scrapers at the slime which had encrusted into scales like chain-mail.

Refilled, it was dosed with costly chemicals which promised to keep it pellucid and pure. Within a fortnight the algae was in great shape again, foaming over the top like a pint of green Chartreuse with a good head on it.

There are, too, other drawbacks. It is, I fear, a death trap for silly creatures which blunder about in the dark and miss their footing. I have pulled out the small corpse of a shrew, its anteater's snout upturned like a blocked snorkel. A mole met its end there, for even those massive bulldozer claws could get no purchase on the sheer slippery stone sides. The saddest discovery was a deceased grass-snake, which must have thought it was crossing a river—but even so sinuous a swimmer and climber could not mount that parapet.

What hadn't occurred to me until this winter is that we have a marvellous home skating rink. I have just been mooching beside it. The water is tea-coloured again. The marble goddess peers broodingly at her dream-like reflection. It is as pensively moody and subfusc as that exercise in Victorian neo-classicism, Frederick Walker's *Autumn*.

I never aspired to being a swimming pool owner. But this year I may leave it to the algae and the dragonflies and the water beetles.

If visitors jeer at the flash decadence of such a possession, they will be challenged. Bikinis and trunks will be provided. Swim in that icy soup and still sneer.

March

THE side of the Knoll overlooking my garden and the river valley shoots up at such a tilt that the few old thorns and a wizened oak struggling up to the sheepwash look like a ropeline of desperate climbers about to fall off backward.

It is a worthwhile scramble, up into the airy world of harebells and gentians beyond the petrified and barkless tree whose gallows bough is a favourite sniper's post for buzzards watching for a rabbit to pick off. The winds thump against the obstruction and swoosh skyward and are intermixed with wafts of warm currents in summer, so then it is a sporting place for birds. Buzzards, kestrels, rooks, jackdaws, woodpigeons and house martins joy-ride on the buoyancy, volplaning down to be lifted again on fanned out wings.

Yet after feeling that you can't be topped up here you see that on the further flank of the dome there isn't the sickening drop you would expect. The land slants flatly down, like the platform of a colossal tipper lorry which has just unloaded the timber pile of Brushwood Copse and slid it into the gulley.

Having climbed the sheer face, and feeling in my usual conquerer-of-Everest mood while at the same time nervously counting my heart beats and sweating despite the biting cold, I saw in the big field below two hares.

They hadn't noticed my lurching arrival. They were

being just as hare-brained as hares are supposed to be in March, mad as a . . . well, typical. In the bright light their fur was a silky henna—the winter grey sexily burnished up—and they were prancing around each other on their hind legs, breaking away into jinking chase, then squaring up again.

Like boxing kangaroos, they were making apparent jabs with their forepaws but never, as far as I could see, connecting. Then I spotted, lower on the plough, another hare, complacently squatted: doubtless the female over whom the two bucks were battling.

By the time the leverets are born the corn will be high enough for concealment and the temperature above the survival notch. How do the adult hares know that it will work out so neatly?

What triggers each wild creature into its individual breeding season still mystifies physiologists. Lengthening daylight, milder weather, increasing food supplies—all probably influence the internal mechanism and the rising of the mating sap.

But the old theory of a biological 'clock' was blown up by Dr. John R. Baker, of Oxford, who showed that, with an annual variation of only six minutes, a spring breeder of the last ice age would now reproduce in the autumn.

It remains a puzzle: how blue tits foretell that by laying at precisely the right period their dozen or so chicks can be feasted on caterpillars which are abundant so briefly.

There must be stimuli too delicately subtle for our clumsy sensory outfits to detect.

What, for instance, arouses passion in a frog? It is the maddeningly provocative scent of a certain algae, activated by New Year rains, which influences its nervous system. That is why they now rasp so amorously through the night in the marshy bit of my garden.

After considerately backing away from the hares, I reflected on the way down that some have it better organized than others. Herons and mistle thrushes and other high-rise dwellers don't need the safety screen of later foliage.

Yet, looking down from the hill into the beech plantation of my own valley, where the rooks were swaying on their stick penthouses in the bitter blast, I could see no point in such impetuosity.

What better, as the poet has pointed out, than 'Love in summer's wonderland'?

*

I drove into Casterbridge with my wife. She had to renew her road fund licence. The motor tax office is one of those modern buildings which look as if they came in a cigarette coupon construction kit, but only up the high street are where Judge Jeffries lodged when holding his Bloody Assize and where Thomas Hardy served his apprenticeship in architecture.

This structure was slotted together opposite the postal sorting office in what was the barrack square of the King's Own Halberdiers and Yeomanry. Now cars park on the parade ground where volunteer musketeers and pikemen trained to resist Boney's imminent landing, when lookouts on the beacon hills around watched tensely for the French fleet's sails (and balloons—it would have been the first airborne invasion), the womenfolk and children of Poorstock were herded to the top of Haggerdown, behind ramparts built a thousand years before, and cattle and waggons were grouped at the foot, ready for evacuation.

The Casterbridge keep was added later—a grey stone flourish of Victorian sham medievalism. The arrow slots have window panes. The block with a semi-det martello tower houses a military museum.

Yellow chimney pots and cement stacks perch on the fortress like a paper hat on a marble bust. A brick row in 'Twenties Tudor has chiselled over its Gothic doors such dolorous campaign names as MONS.

Crouched menacingly around the museum is a sort of Battersea Dogs' Home of artillery—bits and pieces of decrepit missile engines, orphaned field guns with muzzles pointing heavenward in silent howls, strayed coastal cannon, and doleful obsolete trench mortars.

While waiting I sat on a blunt gaping barrel in this almshouse for demobbed death-dealers and watched a more positive approach to life. There is a row of pollarded elms. Defiant young boughs have sprouted where each trunk was beheaded, and formed new coronets.

Two jackdaws had picked on the elms as their supply depot. Rashly—jackdaws don't normally breed for another month—they were gathering nesting material at a furious rate. They had been lured into precipitate honeymooning by the few days of champagne sun, with only the faintest fibre of cirrus cloud in otherwise unblemished blue.

They hopped and fluttered through the bare branches looking for dead ends, tugging and testing. Here was one brittle enough. Clench. Wrench. Crunch. Off it snapped. It was carried crosswise in the beak to one of those yellow chimneys, and the jackdaw dropped down like a potholer with a pickaxe.

Its mate was really rather dimwitted, despite its air of efficiency as it alertly cocked its grey-shawled head at likely material. It kept sidling along whippy branches and trying to break off the part it was sitting on.

Well, other birds already had taken the risk—the rooks in the hanging wood behind the mill and the mistle thrushes, back in the spinney where the cock sang louder than the engine of the tractor pulling a roller over the oblong of barley to firm the frost-cracked soil. Capricious though March can be, the jackdaws were not first off the mark.

Each time the branch bent and the jackdaw continued performing its circus clown act of doing a pratfall in mid air.

I sat working out how many hours of wood-carting

the cleverer bird would have to do to fill that chimney, twig by twig. And I speculated on the chances of someone over there needing a fire—and either getting a bigger blaze than was expected or, twigging, ramming out the pile first.

The jackdaws seemed to me to be squatting in high-risk premises.

Don't ask me why they had scorned a safe arbour in the wide open country around. Cannon to the right of them, cannon to the left of them, a bonfire beneath—some birds choose to live dangerously.

*

Purple was the colour of its plumage. No, that makes it sound as lugubrious as a judge's dewlaps. It was purple glinting with lights like a matador's suit.

As it moved in the sun and the wind ruffled its feathers, the sheens shifted and danced. Peacock blue flashed into a dazzle of green shot with bronze. Brilliant spangles of mauves and pinks shimmered as a sun-ray dodged through wind-blown cloud and spot-lit it. From its lemon-yellow bill to its red legs it seemed a-sparkle with sequins.

What exotic rarity was this which had settled on the barn ridge tiles? What fantastic jungle fowl had strayed from the tropics into my damp valley?

Actually, nothing to send an earthquake through the ornithological world. It was just a common or garden starling, singing its common or garden serenade, which has the melodious euphony of a two-stroke engine blowing a gasket.

It sat on its pinnacle wheezing and rattling and gurgling and spluttering, interspersed with a rhythmical pop-pop-pop. Starlings are mimics. It must have listened admiringly to the moped on which a village boy whizzes into the Port Bredy rope factory every day along the hillside lane.

The starling was, with beak raised to the sky like a

bugler at dawn, sending forth an urgent but indiscriminate love call, an invitation to a house warming. Anyone listening? I saw no rush to join him and I walked on.

Starlings have an exceptional marital custom. The male settles on a site which takes his fancy and he builds the nest. Then he looks around for a mate to do the interior decorating with feathers and leaves, and to provide the pale blue eggs. Bachelor, house-owner, wants to meet serious-minded young woman, view matrimony.

For a week I had been watching this bird ferrying beakfuls of straw—a bit narrow-eyed. It had appropriated a place meant for another. Months ago I sawed a circular hole in the hay loft door and inside fixed a deep partitioned box.

I hoped it might lure a pair of barn owls—the white owl, now so scarce, which floating wraithlike through the dusk has been the origin of many a ghost story—to take up residence.

No owls found it. The starling had. An opportunist and spivvy bird, it nipped in and grabbed vacant possession.

I grieve that no barn owls showed up. There are a few in the district. A pair nested not far away in a ruined lime kiln last spring. And I saw two others quartering the reversed-S bends of quick-set hedges on the rough grazing of North Poorlot, which outline where the common furlongs were enclosed in the mid-1600s. A roofless Tudor farmhouse is tucked deep under the wild heights, and I fancy those two owls shared tenancy with the bats and spiders and swallows.

Barn owls have always, to me, seemed especially beautiful and fascinating birds. I would like to see them fanning through the darkness around my buildings, a sanctuary for them if only they knew it. They would also deal with the rats which scrabble through my compost heap like bargain hunters at a rummage stall.

But as long as the barn stays un-owled, I suppose the starling may as well lodge there. Watching it whistling for a partner, I realized how often the eye passes unseeingly across the familiar sight.

A bit common he may be in all senses, but the starling decorates the gable like a finial ornamented with rhinestones, a winged hippy with self-grown furbelows. Showy, yes. Trumpery—a little. But he certainly cuts a shine.

*

It is a still mild day and from two directions, east and west, drift the sweet love songs. From the spill of beeches down the river cliff and from a straggle of maple and pine along a backbone of field, swelling melodiously come the voices of the rooks.

Sweet? Melodious? Rooks! If such scathing exclamations are being uttered I can only urge that, clearing your mind of careless and prejudiced remarks made in print about harsh croaks, you cock an ear.

Even the peerless Gilbert White wrote from Selborne: '. . . the amorous sound of a crow is strange and ridiculous; rooks, in the breeding season, attempt sometimes in the gaiety of their hearts to sing, but with no great success'. Ah, but he was wrong. Altogether the rook is much wronged.

It gives me pleasure to live between two rookeries, one a sizeable stick city, the other a mere hamlet of seven nests in that hedgerow line. When I was a child of London suburbia, make-believing canal scrub-waste and orchard remnants, lapped by housing estates, into that timeless deep countryside which arose like the smell of buttercups from children's books, most magical for me was the unlikely rook.

Players issued a bird series of cigarette cards. One was a rather floridly coloured photograph shot down into a rookery. Sun struck rainbow glints from glossy black plumage; the stout baskets held brown-marbled eggs.

Why should I remember this so distinctly from forty years ago? Because the branches, still winter black yet stippled with buds, were at furthest stretch into a world of sky and cloud and lucent air. I looked at the cigarette card and dreamed of tree-top freedom in the wind above the ploughland of England.

Although familiar, rooks have never been popular. As long ago as 1424 James I of Scotland commanded their slaughter. They can make a mess of a maize crop and those pickaxe grey bills soon prise out seedling peas.

But they also gobble quantities of wireworms and leatherjackets. Probably the rook is neither friend nor foe of the farmer; merely as is the way of the natural scheme, an element of balance.

It seems to us inseparable from our landscape of churchyard elms and copses on broad arable. Elsewhere it isn't a common bird, even as close as France.

On a Sunday evening at this time down the chain of little valleys comes the pealing of Poorstock's 12th-century church bells—including that No. 5, recast at Cullompton in 1772 and engraved with the unforgettable couplet:

To the Church the Living Call
To the grave do summon all.

Now that chilling admonition passes, assuaged, through the pugnacious life-affirmative broadcasts of chaffinches, wrens—and the rooks.

When I cross the towering ground around Haggerdown—divided by stone walls, hedgehogged with gorse, and the indentations of the iron-ore quarries of the pre-Roman Celts—in the bitterest weather the rook tribe is up there, some perched facing into the gale with smoothly combed feathers, others billowing up like water-skiers across the green waves.

And as soon as the catkins are out the rooks are back at their valley nests. I have been walking around the beech hanger in the sunshine. The cawing was soft and warbling as they flopped about their repaired homes. The rooks were singing.

*

I have never bragged that I possess a flair for cuisine: I don't feel me in one of those striped pinafores men buy in Soho and my hands covered in flour.

Therefore I do find it a mite irritating that raucous laughter is directed at me because when on one occasion my wife deserted me to spend some days gallivanting about West End theatres and Chelsea restaurants I telephoned a London friend at a latish hour seeking help.

I had been striving to prepare some frozen broad beans and could not get them to soften. They dropped on to the plate with the clang of cobbles. Guided by the voice 150 miles away, I managed to coordinate broad bean with boiling water. That seemed to me a rather resourceful way of dealing with the emergency.

Although I do not go in for fancy cooking, I quite enjoy being on my own. Despite the brilliance of daffodils around the millpond and the—there's no other word for it—noisiness of the birds' evensong, it was bleakly chill at twilight. Rain spat, then battered the panes. After busting out all over, spring was locked back in a crypt.

Writing done for the day, I closed the white wooden shutters over the kitchen's long glass doors and bolted the diagonal iron bar—probably fitted to keep out Bonaparte. That was a grave time hereabouts. 'Discreet trusty persons' were instructed to hold these villages as fortresses and our market town raised eighty-four Volunteers under a captain, two lieutenants and an ensign decked out in green-faced scarlet uniforms with silver buttons. When the Colonel collapsed and died all the Volunteers at his memorial dinner were in tears and, it is recorded, the toast to him was drunk in dead silence and 'the only sound that was heard was the bottle passing from one to the other'.

My dinner was noisier. On the wireless Alan Dell was playing big band music from the '40s. The lamp shone on copper-bottomed saucepans, brass dresser knobs and tawny quarry tiles. There's nothing like an Aga for getting a sumptuous fug going.

I fried eggs and bacon (with a confident ease: I have eggs and bacon taped) and dropped the rind into expectant jaws, for the dogs involved themselves in the busy operation by being at hand to tidy up spillages and splashes. Amid piles of magazines and aligned beer bottles, I and the dogs settled into an enjoyable squalid torpor.

The doorbell rang. I thought of crouching under the table, but the light would have been spotted.

It was an old friend, a novelist, not seen for three years; he was back from America and motoring through to Cornwall. We drank some whisky. He insisted that I went out to eat with him. I demurred. I did.

We did not head for that café in a neighbouring town which has 'Venison-and-chips' chalked up in the window for I don't care for the way the roe and fallow deer are mangled by sawn-off twelve-bores poked from the windows of furtively cruising cars. But I confess that we did not take a moral vegetarian stand.

We drove to a Good Food Guide inn on a turret of downland, from where we could see the lights of Somerset and Devon, like earth-bound star galaxies. There we consumed rare and costly fowl and spices and potations. Then we dawdled back through the night in which a white owl floated and the moonlight flooded like whey across the immense hills, the forest and the meadows becoming touselled again with spring grass, to my own valley and a brandy bottle.

I don't in the least mind looking after myself.

*

The dippers have had me troubled in mind. I had counted myself uncommonly favoured to have a pair on the premises. Last spring they built their bulky nest, with its drip-proof moss roof, under the stone footbridge where the stream forks over a waterfall. The fledglings, speckled as young starlings, blundered into the house.

The dipper isn't usually so domesticated. I was used to spotting one occasionally on fast shingly rivers in my native Yorkshire dales or on Exmoor. Here, plump and natty as *maître d'hôtels* in their tuxedo-and-dickey garb, they were always to be seen from a window, bobbing and bowling on the sluice gates or on the boulders below the weir.

There are still bird watchers who are sceptical that this portly relative of the wren can actually walk under water. It does. I have watched mine half diving, half fluttering, pecking with outstretched heads as, completely submerged, they skipped along finding toeholds on the bedstones.

The trick, clearly, is using the current against slanted back to keep it pressed down. How long in evolutionary measurements must it have taken this one-time woodland bird to become so nonchalantly amphibious?

Throughout the winter I now and then saw a dark triangle whizzing upstream. But a few weeks ago it occurred to me that the dippers weren't much in evidence. They breed early and there was no sign of a pair in residence. There might, I thought, be an unpleasant explanation.

I suspected pollution. In late autumn a dead trout came floating down. A lot of the froth and bubble gyrating away from the foot of the spillway looked to me unlike natural foam—to have the synthetic glitter of detergents.

Where did the slops drain to from the washed churns in that farm in the dip under the chalk water table? Into a drain which led to a ditch which led to a rill which joins the brook which is a tributary of the small river whereon my house stands, and which in the course of many a twist and loop, goes to swell the bigger Bredy. I decided that we must gather some forensic facts.

Of course when the River Authority official arrived the froth had gone, like toothache at the dentist's door. He left me jars which I am to fill with samples for laboratory analysis, and I make periodical skimmings which look like bottles of snake-bite lubricant, so tinted and pungent when the stopper is lifted out.

One sharp pointer to pollution is if dippers desert a river, for the larvae and tiny molluscs they eat are killed off by chemicals. It depressed me that the poisons might be filtering through into even these remote chalk hill springs—but today there can be no escape from the pervasiveness of pollution which is presented under brandnames and advertised as agricultural elixirs.

Yesterday morning as I was shaving my eye was attracted by an eddy on the still mill pond. I craned to the window in time to see a dipper break the surface and flip on to the stone sill.

As it perched, curtseying at its white-bibbed reflection in the water, it was joined by another—and they began bowing to each other and shivering their wings in mating display.

Even if toxic strains are filtering in and washing down into the valley the dippers obviously aren't going to be driven out easily.

*

I was trying to maintain a military bearing. It took some doing. But, surrounded by young cadets about to launch the offensive, one owed it to oneself not visibly to quake at weather and terrain.

The colonel jabbed an ash pole at the map, flapping in the gale, while we were pelted with hailstones like small-arms' fire. 'We're here,' he shouted. 'We shall circle to this point.'

No enemy were we after. Our motives were the

friendliest. The fifty of us were on parade (in a huddled sort of way) on the crest above the spruce slopes, recruited to help in the roe deer catch-up. In Poorstock Forest the Forestry Commission annually holds half a dozen round-ups to amass data for a long-term behaviour research project. How long do roe deer live? On what? Where? How far do they range? Are they a pest to farmer and woodlander?

In a country so miniature as ours we perhaps have the vague general idea that we by now have the measure of all our native birds and animals. Yet what do we really see of them beyond an occasional fleeting glimpse? Most of their lives are spent invisible, private, beyond our range of understanding—how little we really know about them.

The Forestry Commission is incessantly lashed for being a brutish open-air factory for pit-props, for blanketing our hills with black, quick-quid conifers. It's fair to mention the altruistic dedication the Commission permits its rangers and staff naturalists to add more to the scanty knowledge of our mammals.

A seventy-strong roe deer herd lives in this beautiful wood, slung like a cloak across the best we can offer in the shape of a mountain: the spectacular plunge from the chalk battlements around my village into the vast lowlands of Outer Wessex. The Commission puts up with the deers' nibbling—although it does curb (by culling) the 'fraying', the hooliganism of young males, which tend, literally, to be tearaways.

A mature buck warns off a rival from his territory with an authoritative bark. 'But one problem,' explained a Chase officer from under his deer stalker's soddened brim as we plodded down the squelching ride, 'is what we call the coffee-bar gang of the less bright young bucks. They do make a mess of the plantation.'

They get into aggros with each other. They 'fray' the saplings in churning gang squabbles.

In the first sweep a seven-year-old, antlers now furry

stubs, was nabbed. A net-watcher threw his anorak over its head. It reclined quite still at the trackside. A Land Rover drew up. Blindfolded and hogtied, it was lifted aboard.

Down in the control hut we watched it having its check-up (temperature, respiratory rate, weight) and its flanks were 'freeze-marked'—patches shaved and follicle-treated so that only white hair will grow and thus mark it. It lay breathing gently, not frightened, calmed by firm, gentle hands.

Crackle of walkie-talkie. 'Demoralization setting in among beaters', was the message from the dissolved distance. No wonder. The hail had turned to snow, then to hissing sleet which whipped across bramble thickets and sandwiches of dead bracken.

Clay paths were awash with yellow goo. Nothing had been seen but a high-flying pheasant and two woodcock. The deer, sensible lot, were lying low in their undergrowth caves.

Catch-up called off. We sloshed off under a charcoal sky—and past a skeleton. Poachers had left on the bright plastic identification collar but had flayed off the flesh. Joints go up to London restaurants—from those killed outright from twelve-bore blasts and which don't hobble off to die in the hollows of infected wounds.

April

YOU can tell it's spring. From the cap of Round Knoll I look upon the April sun, bright as the celandines, glinting with crescendoing power upon scattered farm buildings—every tin inch of them.

Doing a rough sum I calculate that it can't take more than another twenty-five years to rebuild Wessex entirely with corrugated iron.

Primroses cluster around rusty sheets of it rammed in the hedge of Larchcombe Lane. Simpler, isn't it, than filling gaps with thorn slips or by laying the old boughs?

In the next village the mossy thatch was rotting off a cottage. It has been replaced by that asbestos composition like an elephant's wrinkled hide. Of course thatchers are scarce and tiling would probably cost ten times what the whole cottage did originally.

Between there and my mill two sunken rutted lanes cross at an askew swastika junction. It is called Bellbakery. There was once a bit of a village there, gone now but for one cottage, which was the bakehouse and pub. It is the loneliest of spots. At least, it was lonely. I often came that way when homeward bound near dusk.

In the meadows partridges skreaked like rusty hinges on doors parting to let in the dark. From its telegraph post podium a yellowhammer's asthmatic little-bit-of-bread-and-no-cheese trill promulgated its ownership of a patch of furze.

It was at this hour that the barn owls flapped to the ivied rim of the tumbledown lime kiln, blearily peered about through heart-shaped facial feathers, then spread their wings for the night's hunting.

If I leaned quietly at the five-barred gate, they came floating past within feet, thistledown-soft and silent, cream and golden footpads prowling down the fence for a vole or shrew.

That's how it was. The owls and yellowhammers and partridges are still around, but it's hardly the same secluded valley. Now it's the site of a pig farm. And why indeed shouldn't this parcel of land provide bacon for us as well as meat for owls? But need it be so shriekingly ugly? The sties, barns, hutments and food stores, plonked smack dab in the middle, are metal down to the last rivet.

Buildings put up by earlier farmers were like outcrops of the surrounding earth, harmonious, organic, as fitting as the field oaks and the kingcups. Stone was carted from the great Purbeck quarries to construct the grand houses and the splendid church towers in the 15th-century perpendicular style. But most of the humbler buildings on the chalk were made either from cob faced with flint and roofed with wheat-straw thatch, although some were put up with bricks available from the belt of London clay, and roofed with healens, or flagstones, by squires of the more prosperous Georgian period.

Most in my village and around were made of blocks of sandstone cut from the hillsides west of Emminster. (When I was picking some stone to repair a derelict wall, Daniel, who was giving me a hand, said that piece was 'too beefy'. It looked just the opposite to me: too crumbly. And indeed that was what he meant, I discovered. Porous limestone interlayered with shale is called 'beef' hereabouts.) The honey-coloured stone soaked up the sun like flesh and had a rosy afterglow in the half light.

The new structures, like Manned Spacecraft Centres,

don't. Their angular hardness provides no texture for lichens and mosses; no swallows or robins can find nesting places in the pre-fab hangars. Alien and raw, these rootless mass-production units can never become part of the contour of the country.

So the tinscape spreads. Why not use stone and slate and straw? It 'isn't worth it'—meaning that it's cheaper to bolt together the gawky components.

Hovering around these rustic shantytowns, of course, are bodies entitled Rural District Planning Committees. What consideration do they give to standards which are seemly and appropriate to the areas they oversee? Cheapness is all.

*

Throughout the year there is a positive ballet of wagtails running at the mill. They are the most vivacious and capersome birds—but do wagtails maliciously set out to confuse and confound human beings?

I know a pied wagtail, of course, that jaunty black and white minstrel of the barnyard . . . except that you have to bear in mind that it might be a white wagtail. As any self-respecting ornithologist will instantly point out, the pied has a darker rump than the white—needless to say, with the qualification that some young female pied are as pale as whites. And, it must not be forgotten, in autumn first-year pied are eerily similar to adult male whites.

Stifling incipient whimpers, regard instead the grey wagtail. Now there's a handsome bird, streamlined body gilded as a daffodil beneath, which I see on frosty days darting along the stream edge among the brown stems of speedwell and wall-ivy, and perched with vibrating tail on the sluice gates.

Yellow though it is, it doesn't fool me into mistaking it for a yellow wagtail, because the yellow wagtail is yellower and anyway is a summer visitor which keeps to water meadows. On the other hand, a few do hang on here through the cold months.

Or are those which straggle through on migration blue-headed wagtails, also maddeningly yellow? Could they even be the ashy-headed or black-headed, not to mention the grey-headed, which, as everyone knows, is quite distinct from the grey? Your guess is probably better than mine.

Frankly, I'm pretty rough and ready about my wagtails. If I see a yellow one in winter around the mill I reckon it's a grey. And if I see a pied one I assume that it's a pied. Those are the ones which draw a harlequin squiggle across the gloomiest day as they loop, chirrupping, from roof to ground and on to the drystone wall, tail never ceasing to quiver, bright eye peeled for any insect to lance at a running tilt.

A couple of pied seem to be settled on the premises all the year long, but in fact there is probably quite a turnover. Those which dribbled down to the valley last September are likely to have migrated north again, and the pair now in residence may be returned from wanderings far afield.

Last autumn I took a moderate pruning blade to the fig, vine and jasmin which swarmed thick and matted over the big barn, so unruly that the windows were cloaked and the doorway reduced to mouse-hole proportions.

That was where the pied wagtails had nested, in the tangle under the guttering, and I had wondered if they would take to the new, relatively open-plan conditions. Yesterday, as I crossed the forecourt with an armful of kindling I noticed one of them scuttering about with a moustache sprouting from its bill. It was collecting straw and dead stems from the gravel.

Having closed the kitchen door behind me, I went to the window. Believing itself unobserved, the wagtail flitted straight up to the barn and hopped, zigzagging, through the cropped stems and into the old crevice with its nesting materials.

It may be the same pair back at the old homestead. Or these may be replacements with a wagtailish instinct for continuity and the right niche for them.

I was glad to see that. For this attractive bird probably has tough times ahead. E. M. Nicholson, in his *Birds and Men*, points out that this one-time cliff-nester has become dependent upon man-made shelters because of its need for the insect life of shallow waters and the proximity of animals, so it has become a close companion of man 'whom it has nevertheless not ceased to regard with nervousness and mistrust'. Conspicuous though it is, it is not really all that common—and, says Nicholson, with the rapid spread of piped water, modern hygienic cow-sheds and insect-sprays 'it looks as if the phase of civilization which helped the pied wagtail to flourish may be gradually passing'.

There were no pied wagtails down at that tin pig farm at Bellbakery.

*

I have been learning how to be a poisoner. 'I wouldn't use strychnine,' the local expert confided. 'Overkill, as you might say. Pop into a chemist's and get some thallium sulphate. That'll finish her off, no trouble at all.'

I could not bring myself to feel altogether at ease about the plot. I went so far as to get the ingredients. There they stand, poised for destruction. In one container is the lethal jelly. Beside it, another holds the tit-bits waiting to be dosed, a biscuit tin writhing with so far healthy, pink earthworms.

The idea is that I drop the worms into the jelly for three hours, then deposit them in prepared bore-holes. And that—is the plan—will be the end of the mole which has moved in on me.

Was the word molest ('meddle hostilely or injuriously with') inspired by the mole? It must have been. Unfortunately my village counsellor was too busy to take on the job, and Archie, the county's ace mole-slayer, has retired. It was up to cowardly me. Leaving the worms not yet bloated on thallium sulphate, I marched into the garden.

Over the hill crest, where geans are flying white flags of blossom (I saw bees making a bee-line for the new cherry flowers), came a tractor. The driver breasted the high breaker of field like a dreadnought. He was drawing a bush harrow across a field set for hay, riddling the soil to aerate the roots of the young grass and spreading the manure of the dairy herd which has been grazing there. The row of prongs was leaving broad brush-strokes of light and shade as the young stems were stroked one way and then the other in bands. The machine seemed to be casting up a white spray of herring gulls, fluttering on to the disturbed insects.

I felt cynically that the tractor might well have taken my lawn in its stride. It looked like the set for *All Quiet on the Western Front*: a splattered no man's land of minced soil piled in hummocks and pitted with craters where I had tried digging out the enemy.

This one must be an extraordinarily powerful digger. It actually does make mountains out of mole-hills. Perhaps—I pale to think of it—it is a female, as my neighbour suggested. Perhaps she has made her nest of moss-tufts and springy roots beneath one of the enormous heaps, and is constructing a vast underground adventure playground for her offspring.

It was too nice a day to be thinking dark thoughts of murder. The gulls yelped and flashed on the skyline. A blackbird pealed on an apple bough. Two long-tailed tits ransacked the hedge, laced with honeysuckle shoots, for spiders. There are dog violets opening and the starry white heads of stitchwort are pushing through the verge tangle.

I tried sending the mole vibrations of reasonableness, to the effect that I had no wish to wage biological warfare, that if it would sensibly shift beyond the yew hedge it could burrow away like billy-o and I wouldn't care.

But, in my bourgeois fashion, I do like my lawn to be level and have grass growing on it. Boringly conventional, I know, but that's the way human beings are, mole. We don't see life from your angle.

I have done my best to discourage this mole. I put down stink bombs guaranteed to drive it out choking and coughing. They didn't. I prodded the hills and tunnels, having been told that moles cannot abide being disturbed. This one is thick skinned.

My hand is being forced—towards those worms and the infernal jelly. Or shall I first of all try putting layers of holly leaves in the runs? For I've heard that even a mole's walloping great paws flinch away from the prickles. Yes, to hell with the poison—I shall do that.

*

Have you noticed how sly birds have got? A male blackbird swoops like Superman to the topmost brick of the highest chimney and bellows a tough-talking harangue about territory—but slinks away. The moorhens on the mill-pond let the world know whose millpond it is by uttering a loud bicycle bell curr-rup—but where do they smoke away to?

I found out. I was on the footbridge throwing the trout some food. These are the trout not so far poached by the heron which forages the little Angerton river and its tributaries which thread through this spacious chalk littoral piling back toward the Wiltshire plains: an inland seaboard of lofty, sublime cliffs with only tiny trickles to wash around their base.

The trout are untroubled by roaring tides. They grow muscular and long in their pool beneath the shade of brooklime and bullrushes and the dark green awnings of water starwort. The survivors of those dawn burglaries by the heron, when their tranquil vault was staved in by that jemmy beak, have shaken off their winter torpor.

They whammed up through the water to snatch the manna from heaven, now hefty speckled bruisers which barge each other out of the way.

I became conscious of a sharp stare upon me. Without turning my head (for that sends a bird flying) I glanced into the tangle of bedstraw stems and daffodils against the stone buttress. The moorhen humped still as a slipper. Only the glinting eye revealed its tension.

I didn't disturb it. Later, when the pair fed down by the dam edge, I nipped out. Three eggs in the little basket of woven sedges. Now why did the moorhens—shy, flustery birds—pick that spot? The bridge is frequently crossed by human and dog feet. Other moorhens have already bagged the river stretch. But on the pond itself this young homemaking couple could have chosen a dozen clumps of flags and kingcups out of sight.

The blackbirds are again nesting in the big magnolia. Every opening and closing of the front door must shake their foundations. Perhaps the passage light provides the illusion of perpetual full moon radiance.

And nesting within spitting distance, I know, are great tits and dunnocks, grey wagtails and goldfinches, robins and wrens, to name but a few feathers constantly flouncing about.

Yet once they've collected material or food they do a fade-out like jungle fighters to their secret hide-outs.

I do not enquire too closely. No gazumping the property here. There is room for all who fit in so harmoniously—and I suppose I must lump it that the heron, too, has its place, providing it doesn't get too domineering.

*

There could be no argument that this was the season of rebirth, I was thinking somewhat guardedly. Leaning on the rail of the footbridge, where the mill stream comes sliding out of the innards of the house, I watched a remarkable sight.

There had been a huge hatching, an instant population explosion. Above the water, between the steep banks of daffodils, was a rising cloud of aerial dancers, each no bigger than a winged mote of dust but in multiple multitudes. Ten thousand? Ten million? No census could make that calculation.

They were, I suppose, midges. And what is a midge? There are, I gather, more than 150 kinds in Britain. But since the Rev. W. Dereham, Rector of Upminster, in 1713 wrote a great work entitled *Physico-Theology: Or a Demonstration of the Being and Attributes of God, from His Works of Creation*, no one seems to have looked closely at the life history and sex life of the 'vexatious Gnat'.

Women, with the unreasoning passion they direct upon things which bite them, seem especially anti-midge. They have been known to wish them dead and to strike them viciously.

It is a slur upon the mighty midge nation. There is in fact only one type which sneaks through the meshes of stockings and sinks its mosquito-style hypodermic syringe to suck human blood. This species, troublesome in western Scotland, is referred to in one zoological textbook with the comment: 'Its presence in conjunction with that of the kilt is said to have given rise to the Highland Fling.'

There are others which get stuck into caterpillars and moths for a feed. Most, though, sip delicately at nectar and plant juices, gentle vegetarians.

Can I be sure that the legions rising from their larval infancy in my garden's dark pools, where the water voles have their tunnels and marsh marigolds cluster, are of this pacifist nature? No, for there is little guidance to go on. Perhaps shunning all publicity in some university is an eminent midge scholar and specialist who could tell at a glance, but I have not come upon his researches.

Standing there, watching the waves float up from their muddy cradle, I was willing to give them the benefit of the doubt—while remaining unbitten.

They were already serving their predestined purpose. Three wagtails—two pied and a grey—had discovered the feast. They were scampering about the dam wall snatching up beakfuls.

And a small neat bird which had been plunking away in the thicket flitted out and settled on a willow bough overhanging the stream. It had the greeny-yellow tint of the new leaves. The chiffchaff, too, began slaughtering the midges, making fluttering raids into the battalions.

And—as if the message had been relayed by radio waves beyond our sensibilities—charging down the valley came a hungry pack of house martins, newly returned to those colony nests under the gables and gutterings in Poorstock. They fell upon the midges with excited, and gluttonous, chirrups.

All good practical reasons for their existence. I found another: their existence itself. They were vibrant surges of life, rising rapturously into the sun's warmth, throwing lambent reflections upon the water and adding to the radiant air a brief shimmer of beauty.

*

It has been conclusively proved that the crazy aerodynamics and wingloading of the bumblebee ground it irrevocably. Indifferent to such scientific pedantry, uncaring of the reputations of Isaac Newton and the Wright Brothers, three bumblebees (dumbledores down here) were levitating themselves without visible means of support around a sallow bush.

Below the mill race this anabranch of the Angerton throws out yet another loop, a twirling bright lariat which girdles the garden's wild side. I was nosing down there to see if the brown trout—the wild fish of this chalk country, not the pampered rainbow trout in the mill-pond, which at the sound of a footstep on the bridge gather round like pet poodles for titbits—were yet basking in the sun-warmed pools.

On the sallow branches the catkins hung like small yellow pineapples. They were fat as the bees. No, one bee was even fatter. Its tiger-furred body was round as a muff.

Its honey-stomach was filled with syrup from the catkins and blackthorn flowers, a full-blown balloon. It must have doubled its weight since awakening from hibernation. Yet those flimsy unworkable wings went on working.

A grey wagtail swooped past. Watch your step, bees. Get that sleep out of your multiple eyes. Enemy beaks are massing. You would be treacle puddings to wagtails building up energy for the frenzied family rearing ahead.

The bees aren't yet fully operational. The sun had prodded an arousing finger down the shrew's tunnel or through the eiderdown of moss where each had dozed through the frosts. They stirred, quaffed this refreshment, but will probably nod off again until the flowers are everywhere abrim with loads for the pollen baskets on their shanks.

The bumblebee knows only summer. The males die as the leaves fall; the impregnated queen wraps her wings around her and sleeps through the coldness. When the honey begins to flow through the land she sits upon her nest of eggs like a warm feathery hen.

Above the powdery red cliff which the thrust of the current has gouged into a crescent (and where there is a kingfisher's old nesting hole—unused, now, for even down here kingfishers are scarce) the bees burnished the air with golden pencillings. I think they were buff-tails—I'm not sure, for there are twenty-five species in Britain alone.

How frail is the thread which sustains them: the few comatose queens nurturing the seed of their kind within their bodies for the long blank months of danger.

If the bees were exterminated, all flowers—their fertilizing transport gone—would vanish too. Cereals and nuts would be the only fruit left. Man also depends upon that filament of life which must see winter through without withering.

*

What was it, bustling ahead, bottom waggling like an old boy in baggy trousers? Of course—a badger.

Bristly hair shimmered silver in my headlights; there was a whisk of a stumpy white tail. It was low-slung and powerful, a miniature bear.

The lane from Uploopers to the river gwyle, or valley, wriggles from Wessex's midriff downs like a snake. Serpentining, it burrows into a ferny sandstone trench helmeted with high trees.

Rounding a bend, I saw the white tail slewing round the next; I got to that and it was heading down a bit of straight at a thumping trot. I hung back at its own speed. It wasn't too perturbed. It cast a slightly surly glance back, a head with vivid humbug stripes and ridiculously petite ears with shell-pale rims.

Choosing its own time, it turned off. The squat bulk shot up the steep bank with the massive agility of a tank rolling up a parapet. It vanished into what was doubtless an old-established badger's right-of-way through the hedge.

I knew where it was from. There's a stronghold in Brushwood Copse beyond the Knoll. Big burrows look like tube train entrances in the dingles. The mushy tracks which those five-toed pads trample through the bluebells show that it's a sizeable colony.

The country name brock is Celtic; it goes back as long as English settlements. Being a night bird, as you might say, the badger doesn't have much truck with man. Yet it is agreeable to a live-and-let-live neighbourliness, if it can peaceably root around for grubs or young rabbits.

It isn't let live. London fur traders pay £1·50 for the pelt of one of our last larger wild animals. A lot of hands are against it, some bearing spades, others poison.

They die under clubs or in agony from strychnine. And hunts block the setts so that the next day's fox won't hole up. Near here last year a sow badger was sealed up and her gauche cubs were found drowned in the stream below.

There is a village workshop a few miles away which, among its choice range of weaponry, such as traps, snares, nets and catapults—what it advertises as 'sporting appliances and sundries'—sells badger tongs at £3·50 a pair. With these the intrepid sportsman can literally collar the badger, once it has been dug out and cornered by terriers, by pincering its neck, at a safe distance from its jaws, with the four-foot tongs. If it is wanted alive it can then be hoisted into a sack and borne away for an evening's fun baiting it with dogs.

Another factor does the badger no good: more cars. The night after that brief procession down the lane, I was returning late along the B-road.

One badger hadn't made the crossing. Its body, still bleeding, sprawled across the white line. The striped head, eyes open, looked like a mounted trophy.

Poor old brock. Although it's never had very friendly treatment, by being a tough independent character, a ditchcomber and hedge-rummager, for centuries it's got by.

Are there beginning to be too many obstacles for it to get by?

*

They certainly struck it rich! See how it gushes up, liquid gold as the expression goes—but usually about another fluid for which the earth is eviscerated, oil. This well produces something more precious by far.

Of course I mean water. When the last superskyliner has burned into vapour the last bucket of oil wrung from our planet's innards, we shall still last out—if water does. Through a cat's-cradle of culverts and iron pipes our house supply comes from across the paddock. Kingcups fly pennants along the stream's course; moorhens tiptoe through watercress beds like old ladies paddling at the seaside.

Springs from Round Knoll, and the ruched hills beyond, rise and mingle in a dell. It is a strange mazey place where stunpoll trees—old and rotting—have listed in the black sponge. They have grown into hammocks of bark, upholstered with moss and tasselled with ferns, and draped with grey lichens long and wispy as the false beards fathers buy to act Santa Claus.

Ivy dangles like tropical vines; a jay flashes like a parrot. It throbs with wood pigeons' voices, deer drink here. Emerald grass, sedges, rushes and an eight-foot reed made with a bamboo-like stem—ready-made drinking straws—grow under alders, holly and sweetbriar.

It is entranced, a touch sinister: hobgoblin land for children. Now it's dappled with sunbeams and primroses. Later the greenness becomes dank. But everywhere is the ripple and music of clear water.

Not everywhere in Wessex is that so. Valley villages have to fight waterboard schemes to extract from chalk streams millions of gallons a day for factory estates. I worry too about crusty meringues of foam which float down my little river. What is it? I again remember farms upstream where, when churns are being washed out, detergent suds gurgle down the drains and eventually the river.

Once more I call upon the River Authority, patient concerned men who survey our rural life across tidal waves of sludge and sewage. I scoop up the nasty looking spume and despatch it for analysis.

With the chemist's report comes a cheering letter from the young inspector. 'A very clean stream' he reports—the gunge must have been natural organic up-bubbling as the temperature rose.

Our life-line is precarious. Standing on the forehead of Haggerdown you can see the precise edge of the water table, graphically marked across our topography by a dotted line of hamlets and farms built along the 'spring line' to tap the flow of pure water without the bother of digging wells. This rumpled landscape also spouts at many points between the permanent streams, in the rainy season when the water brims up in its subterranean tanks of rock and 'peazes up' as intermittent springs, called lavants across in the eastern heath plains, but known here as winterbourns. There are many villages with that word in their names; so it is the name of Hardy's woodlander.

But the Authority is to continue testing with a twenty-four-hour sampling machine. You can't cherish pure water too much. You can't, either, risk rupturing the strata across which it flows for short-term profits from oil bore holes and mineral drilling.

Water costs one penny per person per week from the tap. What is it worth to ensure that the tap doesn't run dry? That hasn't been priced.

May

A THROATY bark loudening into a chorus of yaps far overhead—an airborne pack of mongrels?—drew my eye from the pad on my knee to a barney in the sky. The cloud formations made a dramatic stage set. The cirrus—'mares' tails' or 'gnats' hair'—were being blotted out by a lower layer of enormous cumulo-nimbus with an anvil form which seemed ready to produce a hammer crash of thunder.

As menacing in looks, a band of herring gulls was converging upon a bird about their size but slower and bulkier. The gulls roam in from the coast on marauding forays, like flotillas of pirate ships.

They have the rakish lines of sloops. Their victim was of man-of-war shape, wide brown wings spread like mainsails as it breasted the wind waves under the sombre canopy.

The gulls cut down in formation, heeling on to its tail and whooping their war-cries. It wasn't a serious set-to. Not too concerned, the other bird furled in all that canvas and swooped into the harbour of the beech hanger.

Excuse enough to throw aside my writing for a spot of investigation I'd had in mind. Where exactly had the buzzards set up home? A fortnight earlier, returning from the village, I noticed one of these stately hawks flapping into the wood on the next valley's flank. Every day since, from my garden, I had seen a pair spiralling over the Knoll with an air of regal ownership.

With a guilty glance at that half-filled page, I vamoosed over the stile. While I laboured up the towering mound of the Knoll the clouds rolled away north and as I crossed the wide dale skylarks were up pealing and bees droned in the new clover, as if time could always be suspended at this shining May moment.

Brushwood Copse spills over the facing ridge, an open sunny plantation of oak and ash and beech. Now it is a cataract of bluebells. They curtain the badgers' holes—betrayed by paths of stems flattened by those clodhopping bear-pads.

It is a good wood for breaking your leg in. It is also honeycombed with rabbit burrows, likewise camouflaged booby traps.

I headed for the row of old pines along the upper edge. That, I calculated, was where the buzzards might be ensconced. With no trouble, I spotted four eyries, blockhouses of boughs constructed under the umbrella roofs.

But were all of them 'derries'—abandoned property? One must have been there years, built on to spring after spring. From sixty feet below it looked massive as an armchair.

Then, as I approached the last pine and was watching two goldcrests fluttering like butterflies, a big rufous bird skimmed furtively away on a yard stretch of wing.

Sure enough, a buzzard's nest in the topmost branches. Was it new? I think so, because among the fallen cones was a fresh casting: the pellet of disposables a bird of prey regurgitates after gulping its meal. It was a wodge of rabbit fur, spiky with bones.

When myxamatosis virtually wiped out Britain's rabbit population, our buzzards starved. They tried to subsist on earthworms and laid infertile eggs. When DDT was being squirted over the countryside like scent in a brothel, more died from eating carrion: birds poisoned by sprayed grain.

But a few hardy rabbits survived and spread again, so now the buzzards are returning to the cliffs along the coast where ravens also breed and the wild coombs squeezed between the majestic lion paws of the chalk-mass. So they keep a sounder balance and again soar in the freeness of the serene evening hours over their ancient land.

*

I am a somewhat shiftless botanist. I like to know what things are. So I make haphazard attempts at being better at recognizing flowers.

While walking over the chalk shoulders or just slouching beside the river I keep an eye open for plants new to me. Most are. For although I'm always ferreting about in textbooks for the identity of some unremarkable. hedge bottom sprig, by next spring I can't remember it. Life is an ever-renewing cycle of surprises.

More often, anyway, I forget to look them up when I get home. By the time it comes to mind, and I go to my windcheater to retrieve the specimens, they are limp, pulpy shreds which would baffle a C.I.D. laboratory.

My pockets are lined like old birds' nests with decayed stalks.

I know that those who are expert about wayside blossoms will not deride my efforts at self-improvement when I say that I have been like Sherlock Holmes (yes, with magnifying glass) on the track of the case-history of a small golden spire picked on the leat bank from among the red campion and greater stitchwort. Now those I did know.

I do know too, that the great reedmace which has colonized the lower leat since the dam was repaired and it refilled with water, is what it is and—despite the chocolate-fuzzed sausage which will be fattening on the female stem in a couple of months—not a bullrush. The confusion is due to the translators of the King James's Bible who misread their Hebrew, to be compounded by the Victorian painter who depicted the infant Moses's cradle floating in a forest of *latifolia* (not at large in the Nile Delta).

But what was that diminutive intruder where the stitchwort grew?

It looked like a dead nettle but their red or white flowers I'm also tuned into. Therefore I was pleased to nail it as the yellow archangel.

Such glorification for so modest a posy! That was probably the fancy of some scholarly rural cleric. The countryman calls it weasel-snout—not so high-flown but an earthily accurate image coined by a field labourer who was reminded by the tapering petal of the nose of an animal familiar to him.

Once I start dipping in my tattered guide I am distracted by admiration for long-dead illiterate ploughmen poets who were also keen-eyed descriptive reporters. They first used the names of bristly ox-tongue and skull-cap and bird's-foot trefoil.

Those tough rootstocks which wrested the harrow from its course were within their working experience and were called rest-harrow; the climber whose shining plumes decorate bare winter hedges was rightly tagged traveller's joy.

As most of my discoveries are the Smiths and Joneses of our flora, I am quite excited when I stumble upon an exotic.

Looking for a marsh tit's nest in the muggy shade of the stream-side elms I found a weird little secret conclave. Like the candles on a witch's birthday cake, clusters of tallow-pale columns stuck out of the damp soil. They were studded with mauvish flowers, kneaded out of glitterwax. Meet the toothwort.

Not a pretty plant, but what a schemer. It has no leaves and no chlorophyll, so lives parasitically on tree roots. Furthermore, underground its stem has lidded traps into which foolhardy insects blunder and are sucked dry by the stealthy toothwort.

The juice was once thought to ease toothache. But our forebears, I suspect, had an inkling that that fanged appearance hinted of sinister habits.

So I go on learning what has been common knowledge for centuries in the English countryside, where the classroom has no walls.

*

On one side of the mill my fork of the river bifurcates again and runs into a bough-roofed ravine. Ferns lap the coffee-coloured water. To reach it you have to force your way, Chindit-fashion, through barricades of neglected copse. You heave at palisades of bramble. You wade across a spongy mattress of rotten fallen branches.

I seldom do. It depresses me so. I am overwhelmed by all the clearance I haven't done. Guilt piles up in layers like those leaves of autumn upon autumn.

This time I went altruistically, on behalf of the moorhens. A month ago I noticed that a pair, the silly billies, were anchoring a houseboat of dead reeds on to a half-sunk log.

I feared for them and their domestic aspirations out there in mid-stream. For the nest was perilously exposed. When next I battled over for a quick look there was a splash as the sitting bird slipped off. The half-dozen freckled eggs were distressingly conspicuous. I couldn't see them lasting.

I felt no self-satisfaction at being proved right when, three days later, I saw a magpie swoop out of the shrubbery and flip across the fruit cage with what looked nastily like a biggish egg in its bill.

Once more I pushed through to the river. Sure enough, the moorhen's home had been sacked, bust wide open. A solitary egg remained (one more snack to be called for) and a broken shell dangled from a twig.

It made up my mind about the magpies. In my dithering way I had done nothing since realizing that a pair had had the cheek to settle in the dense juniper growing tight against my writing room window.

For such a flash Harry, the magpie can be amazingly unobtrusive, but I'd glimpsed them sidling up into the juniper with the furtive air of squatters.

I really rather like the magpie. It is a spry and jaunty ruffian which gives a dash of swaggering colour to the scene. But, like all its crow relatives, it is a terrible murderer. At this season, when raising its own young, it keeps plump by plundering other birds' eggs and chicks.

This couple had already been preying on the mistle thrush which built high in a nearby sycamore. Twice, hearing the alarm clock rattle of the thrushes, I had spotted the magpies nosing hungrily around the nest.

I interfere as little as possible with the way things are. No weed-killers go on my lawn, no chemical squirts touch my vegetable garden; and I like to think that my grass is as green as any and that my cabbages and beans, enriched by rotted-down compost, taste even better than most.

So with birds. If bullfinches pluck off some buds, well, I think, the fruit trees can stand it. The tawny owls which breed in the hanger and the kestrels which hunt the paddock, impose perfectly adequate controls upon the local rodents.

Still, just now and then a minor intervention, a spot of habitat-management, is required, and the magpies had brought the matter up.

What to do? Well, I could lift down my dusty shot-gun and blast the magpies to kingdom come—in theory. Actually, I knew that they are better dodgers than I am a marksman.

I took an easier course. Butting my way into the interior of the juniper, I climbed up to the big twig bundle in the whippy top branches.

Before bashing in the stick roof, I scooped out the

magpies' eggs from the deep mud cup and dropped them to the ground, which seemed fair do's.

They might feel unwanted. It would prod them to go elsewhere. It would, on balance, mean many more less bullyragging birds around the premises.

*

Food has never been all that important to me. I wouldn't cross the street in pursuit of some dish extolled by those journalist voluptuaries who champ their way through London's restaurants every night.

Why waste time rolling wine around your gums, inhaling it and crooning over it, when you could be swilling the stuff?

Simple things suit me—a rough-and-ready lobster and a few beakers of Chablis, say. No, gormandizing does seem to be misspent time. But there are exceptions.

When I moved down to Wessex a new delight entered my life: Blue Vinny. It is my staple midday fodder. It is paradisal. I heap this divine cheese in moist mounds upon Bath Olivers, and consume it with raw onion and a glass of red plonk.

Its aromatic richness seeps through one's veins. There is an afterglow lasting hours. The hairs on one's wrists are springier.

In an 1888 glossary of our dialect which I have 'vinny' is given as 'mouldy or mildewy from damp or fungus; blue mouldy cheese'. I suppose it can be reduced to that brutal analysis. At its finest it is, I swear, nobler than Stilton.

It does vary. It can be dry and dusty—then it's called 'chock-dog'. Or it can sometimes be a bit 'bulky', or sharp on the tongue. I'm told that it is vital that each individual cheese is made from the milk of one individual cow, and that must be a beast of singular merit. A factory tried turning it out. It failed. This subtlety is beyond machine mass production.

Of course the character of a local skim milk cheese depends not only upon inherited knowledge of when to drain the whey and salt the curd layers, but upon soil and pasture and climate.

Once there were scores of local varieties of cheese made throughout Britain with flavours and textures peculiar to each region, and doubtless many were pretty chewy, coarse fodder for medieval palates. But why did Shropshire cheese vanish? Why did Kent and Essex lose the knack which once placed the county names like coronets on their product? Surely, Banbury should not have decided to put all its energy into cake-making and allowed the cheese of that sobriquet to become obsolete?

Still, I am consoled by the unique smatch of Blue Vinny.

Wild garlic grows thick down here. The white flower stars appropriately stink to high heaven. If a herd gets among garlic, next day's milk is tipped down the drain. It gives a tang to the cornflakes and tea people don't fancy. My theory is that this pungency seeps through into the cheese.

It is likely that you have never tasted Blue Vinny. I made enquiries in London; Fortnum's don't stock it; Harrods once did but can no longer get it; Selfridges don't have it.

Paxton and Whitfield, in Jermyn Street, obtain some now and then, but know of only two sources. 'And,' said the manageress, 'they guard the secret so closely that they won't pass it on. It's a dying cheese.'

I was filled with dread. Even here, in the ancient motherlode, it is like striking a seam of gold. When I was originally trying to sniff it out, an empty-handed grocer sighed: 'There was a young woman near Emminster who made lovely Vinny, but she married and moved. There's somewhere at Sherton Abbas you can still get it—if you know the right approach.'

You see in what a ticklish day-to-day state of tension the Vinny addict lives. I eventually discovered a small dairy where the sublime cylinders fragrantly moulder. Even the serving girls don't know where they come from, only that they are delivered by someone from Ivell.

He is merely a go-between, a front man. I often think of an anonymous van scurrying under cover of darkness through our twisting lanes, priceless cargo cloaked by an old tarpaulin, the driver's eyes alert beneath hat brim for lurking cheesejackers.

But I have no scruples where Blue Vinny is concerned. Like Chicago's citizens during Prohibition, as long as I get my supply of the real stuff I ask no questions.

*

Living in a house encircled (as well as bisected, not to say permeated) by water can give you Crusoe delusions.

There (goes the fantasy) you can idle away the days playing desert island discs. You can scribble on a bank where cow parsley blows like lace curtains and swallows skim. You can wander over the clover fields with only cloud-shadows as companions. You can tap a nail into the old cart-lodge's sun-warped plank or read books on political-science with the judicious eye which distance gives.

You can even remind yourself of your luck at being that distance from one kind of London life by occasionally flicking an eye at those columnists who write columns about their husbands (also columnists), children (not yet columnists) and their friends who write columns.

But, as I said, a delusion. The river's not much of a moat. Where it is no more than a streamlet it runs over shingle spits, so shallow that the trout have to queue in single file to get round.

Nevertheless, I thought it would keep in my dogs. Not the beagle, for she is unhinged and would free-fall from the Severn Bridge or bound up Everest if the notion took her. The dachs are the surprise.

Previously Tilly, the bitch (I wanted to call her Sweet

Chariot, because she swings low, but she became Matilda) was an animal of astonishing inertia, who frowsted away sunny hours in her slummy basket, aroused to eye-rolling alertness only by the scent of food.

Her son, Duffy (Macduff, for she had a bad time and he was from her womb untimely ripp'd) is not, I fear, the most intelligent dog. He has no inner resources, no soul. His flat pebbly eyes gaze vacantly at nothing.

At least they did lethargically stay put—until moving to Wessex.

There something in the breeze reached their dulled nostrils and stirred in their blood a tingle of ancestral memories: the sniff of badger.

For, of course, the Germans originally evolved the dachshund's torpedo shape to scout on behalf of their owners in their dismal 'sport' of digging out and killing badgers.

With no encouragement from me, Tilly and Duffy have reverted to type. Off they slink, the portly matron gone wrong and the mentally-retarded delinquent. They hate getting wet but lust overcomes their finickiness, and they rush through the river at one of twenty unfenceable points to go scorching fanatically across the Knoll to the badgers' tunnels.

Sometimes they are missing all night. They return gaunt with hunger, exhausted by hysterical excitement, and caked with soil—also, sometimes, with blood from nips.

They frequently have to be sought, for Tilly tends to slip a disc, and has to be strapped into a stiff corset, which gives her the foolish appearance of an armadillo with a black-and-tan head. I have just, again, been tramping among the bluebells and foxgloves, and along narrow paths through the bracken and bushes incised by the hooves of roe deer—a delightful way of passing the time had one not been listening for faint primeval yelps from the middle earth.

I found them tottering home across the meadows.

Unmoved by their craven tail-waggery, I heartlessly left them to wade through mud and torrent, whining miserably now that ecstasy had ebbed, and went back through the gate to seal up my punctured bubble of peace.

*

Outside my window a pigeon is working itself up into a lather. Nervous collapse is imminent. It struts like a Grenadier drill sergeant. Its neck is curved as a drawn bow. Its chest bulges with simmering aggressiveness. It pounds the balcony tiles with pink feet. From its throat comes a furious rumbling. It is spluttering with foiled rage.

'When did it stop being a working mill?' friends ask. I always reply, with a slightly peppery note, that it still is. Corn hasn't been ground on the premises since the First World War—but, by heavens, I say, as I eye my littered desk, work is still done here.

When earlier occupants were doing it up a bit, for some rum reason they screwed a full length looking glass under the balcony's gabled end. (Surely no one dressed out there?) It is in front of this that the dove is posturing and blustering. He is confronting a rival cock, of equal swaggering belligerence, which matches his every move.

When he bristles his nape and hackle feathers this intruder is not intimidated. Indeed, his nape and hackle feathers bristle as fiercely. Clearly it wants to pick a quarrel. A peck of the beak is returned, bang-bang-bang and tip-for-tap.

Well, he must work out some manner of co-existence with his mirror image. After all, he's got it all his own way in the barn loft. In that mêlée of sexual challenging and clashing, the bullying and browbeating on perches and coping, this one is cock-of-the-walk.

How, I wonder once more, did the dove become the emblem of peace? These snow-white purity symbols bicker and duff each other up unwearyingly. After my failure to get a colony going in the clapboard eaves the new lot are bumptiously at home.

They walk into the kitchen. They hunt for spiders in my office. They chase the dogs. And they multiply as though they'd never heard of the population explosion problem.

Of course the old practical purpose of a dove-cote was to crop it: tender, toothsome squabs to go under baked crust.

I am too mushy-hearted for such domestic business. It is pleasant just to see them sunning themselves on the roof slates, so lichened and so saggy, to watch them rise to exultant wings. They hurl into graceful acrobatics through the shining air above the valley tree-tops, before swishing down to their attic where the boss can take out his reflected frustration on the youngsters, cock-pecked as well as henpecked.

*

Kale is all right in its place. That is inside the tubby bellies of those sumptuous beige sheep grazing the stone-walled uplands with their lambs.

What is not its place is growing along Haggardown's arched spine, above the tumuli and hut circles, and eight hundred feet above the blue dazzle of sea.

This rooftop of turfed limestone is a place for kestrels and orchids, for butterflies like flecks of the sky itself, the chalkhill blue and the Adonis blue. They waver among the scabious and harebells, vast as angels against the miniaturized woods and barns on the unfolding tracts below.

This is the grand soaring finale to the westward drive of chalk, the furthermost tip of the arrowhead plateau which narrows across half England from its widely-splayed base points, one in north Norfolk and the others on the High Weald of Kent.

On this last great limb, a dominion of wind, cloud and turf, there is a sense of pure form and power of rock-formation which I have felt nowhere else. Ahead, the vale of clay dissolves into the Devon border.

Sitting quietly here you can see a fallow deer in the rough dell far beneath. Buzzards idle over the oaks of King John's hunting preserve. The wind which planes the flesh from your cheek-bones blows meadow pipits down into the gorse scrub.

This is the great inland promontory about which Andrew Young wrote:

> *. . . there on the hill-crest*
> *Where only larks or stars look down,*
> *Earthworks exposed a vaster nest,*
> *Its race of men long flown.*

A newer race can now roar in high-powered tractors brilliantly marked as Formula One machines and capable of surmounting one-in-two slopes. They slice up those majestic flanks. The kale looks as daft here as would hollyhocks in a window box. The best bit of news from Whitehall recently has been the revocation of Government grants for ploughing virgin land—but there is still encouragement to get at high ground.

It is painful to contemplate the damage done in just this part of Wessex by non-selective cash hand-outs luring ploughshares into old sward, the 'living garment' as W. H. Hudson called it.

Since the 1952 Ploughing Grants Enabling Act, seventy local downs, headlands and hilltops have been done over —and, in the process, irreplaceable ancient green lanes, ridgeways and sheep droves wiped out.

It is no good, I suppose, setting one's face against the post-war agricultural mechanical revolution which has boosted food production. But the strip-and-exploit policy, gone at with such zest, went too far—and not with the stupendous benefits forecast. Some farmers, uneasy at dustbowl scouring on East Anglian prairies, are now resowing quickthorn where were the hedges they grubbed out. 'Intensive methods', 'maximized production' and so on may mean intensive and maximized trouble—and in the meantime so much irrecoverable beauty gone for good.

I can still descend Haggardown's steep snout on a track probably used by prehistoric settlers, but the footprints of the past are fainter.

*

As the slow, late twilight seeped in, dank as bilge-water (we shouldn't expect too much, should we?—still three weeks to midsummer) from the ravine trees, huddled still in only flimsy shawls of leaves, came a fittingly chilling squawk.

The solo became a choir: shrieking and cheeping and gurgling and howling.

I couldn't see them, but I would have snapped up the prize first round if this had been a Mystery Voice challenge. These were our yearly breed of young tawny owls trying to hoot: nursery tantrums because their parents hadn't air-lifted them enough food.

In that decrepit jumble of timber, where trunks are like colanders from the beak of green and great spotted woodpeckers, the owls get busy breeding long before the thought crosses your mind, even in flurries of February snow.

The juveniles are flapping about the branches before the flycatchers and willow warblers are back in the orchard. I know when there are young. I see the parents urgently hunting the tussocky wedge of garden where the river forks rejoin, velvety shadows fanning about like cloaked assassins with daggers.

Three weeks ago a friend returned across the rough ley land from Poorstock Forest with a nestling, tumbled from an invisible crack in one of the gnarled miniaturized bog oaks. The owlet was round as a doughnut, and clad in dingy cotton wool. Now it has swelled with good living to three times the size, and wings around the old stable like that turkey on a wire in the Marx Brothers' *Room Service*.

None of the 100,000 pairs in Britain (it is our most successful bird of prey) has had a better matrimonial start than the Poorstock waif. Being a doctor, my friend was strictly correct with its diet.

Why has it done so well? Because the tawny, unlike its more beautiful but dwindling relative the barn owl, is an adaptable bird which has learned to live off sparrows (even haunting bird-tables) in cities just as comfortably as it does off mice in the country.

Because owls need fur and roughage for their digestive process, my friend prowled about the fields plucking sheep wool from barbed wire. He decided that his small daughter's hair needed cutting, and the snippings, wrapped around chunks of best beef, went down the every-ready gullet.

During surgery hours his wife—who doesn't even like birds—was charged with the important duty of chewing slices of meat to the right consistency and regurgitating them for the owlet's delectation.

But at such a rate has the owl, and its appetite, grown from all that exclusive ministering, that my friend did a rather grisly Burke and Hare deal with a local bird battery manager . . . all those unfortunate sub-standard day old chicks!

Soon the owl will be off fending for itself. It has a rude shock coming. Where will it find fillet steak, medium rare, lurking in the undergrowth? And I hope for its own sake that it hasn't developed an insatiable relish for young chickens.

*

I knew that walk. It wasn't the first time I'd had that rear swaying along in front of me. Instantly I recognized the sinuous swing of long, slender legs, the rippling of hips, like Jane Fonda's.

But down here in the back of the green beyond a Bunny Girl is a female rabbit and the phrase sex symbol brings to mind only the Cerne Giant, that famous (infamous to some tremulous females) pagan and aggressively virile figure carved, possibly seven thousand years ago in the chalk hillside to the north.

Frankly, the throb I felt at the sight of that sleek behind was not one of pleasure, but of exasperation. The buxom Jersey cow was merely the last in a straggling line blocking the lane with a leisurely flood of dipped mulberry and white hide.

To get to the main line station it's a fifteen mile drive. The first four after leaving the mill are up sunken lanes which stripe the car's sides with red mud. In places it is like trying to get toothpaste back into the tube.

We live dangerously hereabouts. Rail go-slows and work-to-rules are not the only hazard. The cows need also to be taken into account. When planning to go anywhere you consult not merely the ABC but also the LMS (local milking schedules).

The Uploopers dairy herd had been put in the high fields where acres of lovely Zephyr barley used to blow, but now rotated back for grazing. I thought I would beat them to it when I headed for that distant express, and drive up the ferny subway climbing to the dairy paddocks. But no—there they were, emerging from the gateway ahead to start their long dawdle to the sheds.

One gets philosophical. I did not sit with revving engine, chewing my fingernails. Resigned, I inched along, gazing ruminatively as a cow.

I looked at the bluebells and buttercups and lady's smock and sanicle along the verges, arranged like a Constance Spry gala arrangement. Songs of blackbird, chiffchaff and cuckoo drifted in the window. My first red admiral of the year toured young nettles.

A leveret, ears absurdly big as a donkey's on its skinny

body, briefly joined the procession. It blundered out of a gap and lolloped between my bumpers and the cows' tails before swerving off up a hare branch-line.

On this grey May morning early hawthorn flowers craned upward looking for the sun, like the city-pale faces of newly arrived campers at the seaside resort failing to substantiate its place in the sunshine league. I also glanced upward and saw a kestrel—still called a vanner ('fanner', I suppose) hereabouts—parachuting with eager talons on to its unfortunate breakfast in the hillside tussocks: a shrew probably which didn't at that last tick in its life-span know it was on anyone's menu.

Wasted time? No, a time of gain.

With a few shouts and flicks from the cowman, the herd jostled into the farmyard and I accelerated forward towards the coastal dual carriageway, anxious again about that train.

I needn't have worried. It was, would you believe it, late.

June

IF a psycho-analyst ever worked me over with a word-association test and threw out 'summer' for a starter, he would get an entire scenario in response.

It is a sultry afternoon. No sun. There are big castles of alto-cumulus which press the heat down. Elms bulge with foliage over a broad lawn. Unstirred by the faintest breeze, the leaves are draped heavy-layered as blankets on a bed in winter.

A faded rope hammock is slung between two apple trees. I've been mucking about in it, trying to spin it round like a chair-o-plane. Now I'm sprawled half asleep, gazing up through seaweedy greenness, thick and suffocating, to patches of light. The sky has become a pewter lid clamped heavily over the soupy stillness.

Part of the stillness is the drone of insects, a dynamo hum, but nearest is the sawing rasp of grasshoppers in the awns where bryony scrambles out from the untidy garden hedge. There is also a thin grating call—attached to the only movement in the dream-like languor. Repeatedly a sparrow-sized bird with streaked pale breast darts out, whirligigs up to snatch a winged ant, and swoops back to its launching-pad twig.

The scene is fixed in childhood, at an aunt's house. Is it a mosaic of different visits? Did one moment etch itself in my mind forever as the very photogravure of mid-summer?

I can't tell. But that bird—a spotted flycatcher, I later knew—became for me an essential presence in the year's high noon when gardens are overblown and stupefied with scents. Amid the torpor the flycatcher is a sprite, mousily plumaged yet whose vivacity puts a pulse of electricity through the air.

Last autumn I knocked together a nesting box with a shelf-shaped bowl and nailed it to the lime whose boughs fan across the grass to the mill stream. Flycatchers like a lookout on the edge of a clear hunting space. I hoped my ready-made flat might persuade a pair to spend the summer with me.

By the middle of May none had turned up, and I forgot about it. This week through a window my eye was caught by an antic twirl of fawn wings. As if it was that moment of forty years ago returned, I watched the flycatcher corkscrew and flicker down upon a cabbage white butterfly and heard that finger-nail-scratching-glass call.

With its catch pincered in its bill, it swished over to the lime: a little spasm of bright energy against the green lassitude where a woodpigeon was groaning with boredom.

Since then two flycatchers are hunting over the lawn, all through the day up to the long twilight, spry air aces who seem never to muff an attack. Once that brilliant eye has fixed on a passing crane-fly, dodge though it might that crane-fly is (you might say) a dead duck.

They are now building a nest: a furious freighting of shreds of lichen snatched from the pear trees, cobwebs plucked from under the loggia supported by the huge oak pillar which was once the axis of the dismantled mill wheel, and (what spondulicks!) combings from the dogs' coats which had snarled up on the rose bushes.

Where did mine come from on those fast but frail wings? Natal, possibly, or even Asia, and it will be a brief stay.

By September's end they, and their young, will have

flown south on their ten thousand mile odyssey—such an outlay to make an English summer complete.

*

Music. Laughter. Lights. 'Knock three times on the ceiling' went dinning around the encircling hills, already a golden oldie as a folk song. The sheep browsing on a patch of surviving slait, or down kept as ewelease, below the Harrow Way (the pre-Roman ridgeway which crosses the Southland from Axmouth to Kent) bleated irritably.

This isn't normal night life in my local town square. Usually the brightest spot is the Washeteria, with its peculiar heliotrope glare. There may be throaty revving from the swashbuckling motorbikes of some loitering Hell's Angels, Wessex chapter. Oftener most row comes from some skyway hell's angels, the summer packs of swifts which hot-rod, screeching, over the Tudor-to-Victoria slate roofs at dusk.

Now the fair has just been occupying the space between white Georgian doorways shawled with clematis and wistaria, and the lollipop-windowed Midland Bank (even finance has a rustic look down here: a piggy bank).

Frankly we can't accommodate much in the way of Big Dippers around the tiny five-spired market cross (1906 'medieval'). It's very nearly a one-coconut shy. There must have been anxious conferences about whether a companion dodg'em car could be squeezed in for the other one to dodge.

It was a gay, gaudy electronic night out—but probably tame stuff after the frolics the town had when Edward I granted its trading charter. There used to be twice the present population, serving the four-story linen factories which worked the flax from the downsides. We forget that villages have dwindled, that the countryside is quieter today.

Entertainment has gravitated to the county's bigger centres, which you might think were Monte Carlo and Las Vegas, not to say Sodom and Gomorrah. My eyes widen at the range of whoopee offered farmers with a night off—and not only the excellent jazz musicians brought down to the Port Bredy hotel.

There in the local paper, alongside 'Buy your new baler now', are such attractions as Wessex's 'top night club' in Hardye Arcade, Casterbridge: Topless Go-Go Dancers, Comedy and Drag, Strip Night with Zirken and Belle.

Over at Ivell, Maggie's Club advertises 'girls in mini skirts free', and a few streets away there's the Tatler Cinema Club, with such milestones of the silver screen as *A Piece of Her Action* and *Hot Nights on the Campus*.

By the village bus or Land Rover you could take in, at half a dozen towns, *The Subject is Sex, 1001 Ways to Love, Love Variations, School for Sex, She Lost Her You Know What, Thigh Spy, Sex Can Be Difficult* and various Swedish exports which cannot be graded as dairy produce.

I notice that, also in Ivell, and no more than one of Lord Longford's strides away from where *The Sex Seekers* is on, the folk club is appropriately presenting Fred Wedlock. Ivell keeps its old people in mind, too. At the Odeon *Run, Virgin, Run* has a 'specially reduced price for Senior Citizens up to 4 p.m.' Who wants to spend the evening of his days polishing horse brasses?

All these goings-on wouldn't have gone on in the days of Archdeacon Thomas Sanctuary: a cleric of singular robustness who not only himself farmed the glebe lands which went with his benefice, and laid roads to carry carriages, but converted the errant with bare knuckles. It was said that he was chosen for our Godless parish while reading Theology at Exeter College, Oxford, where he also obtained a boxing Blue. When the heathen and wanton had been bashed back into line, he kept in trim by taking on the Irish navvies building the Chalk Newton to Port Bredy line in the late 1850s. The

Archdeacon wouldn't recognize the Wessex of today.

I feel such a yokel when I step off the London train into this steamy Soho of the West Country. But I confess that the event which most captured my imagination was on at a pub in Marrobourne, 'the ancient game of Dwile Flonking.'

To my chagrin it had happened before I spotted the announcement. Now I may never know how one flonks a dwile.

*

Every few weeks—when I remember—I clean out the upper leat. This is the section of the mill race which runs deep between stone embankments up to the house wall, providing the head of water which once drove the wheel. Out of the other side it bubbles into the long, low pond where I renewed the dam.

I rather enjoy this job. It gives me a feeling of expertise.

I climb the wooden steps and walk along the levee. The main flow crashes thunderously down the spillway of the overfall weir. The branch to the house is regulated by a curved bulwark inset with sluice-gates which can be slid up or down—or could be if the handles didn't come out of the damp wood like bottle-openers out of rotten corks.

Still, there's another way of imposing one's will upon the upper leat. At right-angles to the sluice-gates is a draw-door weir. This heavy oak slab can be cranked up in its frame by a handle, notch by notch up the rusty ratchet.

As you stand on the plank bridge the pent-up water goes hurtling under your feet down the steep staircase with terrifying velocity. It splashes the ferny wall which hid the grey wagtails' nest and hits the pool, where trout idle, like the dam-busters' bomb.

The ancient master weir, two meadows away, can

cope with normal spates, but it's as well to be watchful. On a wild night last winter a considerate telephone call from two miles upstream warned us that the level was rising fast and building to a dangerous weight.

At midnight I donned waterproofs, battled through the elements to the bridge, slotted on the iron handle and, muscles creaking and lashed by rain, began winding up the door to empty the chamber.

Furtively I quite enjoyed the crisis. I was the man the villagers were counting on to wrestle the dread torrent off its course of havoc.

Usually it's a less pleasingly dramatic task. At this time of the year brown algae balloons, festeringly, up to the surface. It is my squalid chore to scour it out.

I hoped I could recruit my daughter. As I turned the handle and the water sank we saw revealed a huge slimy bulk slithering under the scum.

'It's a crocodile—a dead one!' she whinnied cravenly.

'Nonsense' I said briskly, 'just a clump of pond weed.'

She had gone. Once again, it was up to me alone—down there in the dank pit scraping what smelt like old cabbage from the concrete. But there was much to divert me as I rested—frequently—on the handle of the spade, for during these bountiful summer months the mill stream is a self-service counter for throngs of consumers.

On the menu for the moorhens and dippers (who don't mind getting wet) are pond skaters, water scorpions, horse leeches and the silver water beetle (really it's black but seemingly encrusted with pearls—the air bubbles stored among its fine hairs).

Caddis flies, may flies and the big pillar-box red sympetrum dragon-flies which accelerate up to forty knots to snap up a mosquito, and damsel-flies, which shimmer under the alders, are in turn hawked by wagtails, and by house martins and swifts from the village. The canteen doesn't close at nightfall. When the daytime hunters—and hunted—have folded their wings to roost, others whizz through the starlight.

After long enough at the scraping, I straightened my aching back and stretched my legs up the lane—and looked for a hedgehog. The previous evening it had been squealing with rutting-season ecstasy as it chased a female through the hogweed. Don't ask me how the male mates without being cut to shreds.

No hedgehogs. But the river bank—like an esplanade strung with Chinese lanterns as a dozen moons bobbed winking in the ripples—was busy with traffic.

Bats. Pipistrelles, I thought. They might have been the Daubenton's, which hangs around water (it's often been taken on the fisherman's fly), or the whiskered bat, also among the midgets of Britain's fourteen species.

What do bats get their teeth into at that hour? Plenty. There are, needless to say, lepidoptera; but, needful to say, they may not be only moths. Many moths are abroad in sunshine, from the frumpish little marbled clover to the gorgeous hummingbird hawk moth, and conversely butterflies occasionally stay up late. I've seen a red admiral battering at my gate lamp at midnight.

Mostly, though, it is moths the bats pick on—those and may-flies and daddy-long-legs, and the cockchafers and dor beetles which lumber through the valley's warm night air.

Shamefully little is known about our bats. If you reply that's because you can live without an intimate relationship with bats, well, it's best that we all do.

Bats are declining alarmingly. Why? Because of ever more 'efficiency' in land usage. Forest management dictates that hollow trees are felled. Concrete and asbestos buildings replace old barns. Quarries and ponds are filled. So insects and shelter vanish—and many bats die, too, from overdoses of pesticides.

Ironically, attempts by nature clubs to gather data by ringing probably do most damage. For when disturbed during hibernation a bat's body temperature soars, its accumulated fat burns up, and it cannot survive the winter.

One colony of greater horseshoe bats in a nearby cave fell from 250 to fifty in ten years because of invasions by well-intentioned ringers.

I was content to sit beside the shiny clean leat and watch them.

*

The yellow-rimmed eye was on us. The hard burning glare pierced the thin leaf screen, explosively dangerous as the point of a pistol.

I wouldn't like to be a thrush or a jay on which that ravenous and lethal gaze focuses. But it was a rare treat to be able to watch, without alarming it, the hen sparrow-hawk brooding her eggs.

My friend's cottage is perched like a peregrine's eyrie above the valley. It is altogether a good hawk place. Kestrels patrol the opposite col below the Haggerdown salient. Near here we used to see a pair of Montagu's harriers drifting across the wild scrub of their top-secret nesting place. And over the brow of the hill we watched two hobbys having contemptuous games with a buzzard, cutting it up like two Spitfires making rings round a Heinkel. Then last spring he suspected that two sparrow-hawks had set up in business in the wooded gully. He had occasional glimpses of a bullet-shape skimming the bottoms seeking a bird to drop. This year he found the nest, and took me to see it.

A solid basket of boughs was jammed in the fork of an ash, washed around by a wild crab-apple's sudsy blossom. We squatted in a bramble clump over a row of 15th-century strip-lynchets. Across the cup, where orchids raised purple spires among the water mint, it was only forty yards in a level line to the hawk's home.

She was off the nest when we arrived but a wren's alarmed stutter revealed that the killer lurked in the undergrowth. We waited quietly, field-glasses trained.

Suddenly, with a vault, the hefty gunmetal hen, with

a chest of football jersey stripes and gangly lemon legs, was crouched on the edge. That terrifying glitter scanned for enemies. We froze. She hopped forward, fluffed out her feathers and gently spread her body's warmth upon the next embryonic generation of her kind.

They are needed. For the sparrow-hawk went into catastrophic decline ten years ago when crops were being drenched with toxic chemicals.

The finches they caught finished off their foe with the pesticides in their blood. In expanses of Britain the sparrow-hawk became extinct as the dodo. It managed to hang on in the clumpy hollows here in Wessex, and now seems to be recovering.

The peril hasn't passed. As we circled back to the lane we saw a sinister figure—hooded, canister on back, hosing the hedge bed and the cornfield balks with a metal spray gun.

So much easier than scything: death by defoliation, leaving nettles and wild plants shrivelled and brown. Yet it is a strange, ugly role into which manufacturers' salesmanship has lured the farmer: the husbandman poisoning the land traditionally in his care, upon which he and we live.

*

Not being equipped with electronic beam automation, or even one of those finger-tip flaps which glides up like a visor, the garage stayed unused.

It was so tedious climbing out of the car and heaving open those two great warped barn doors under the pigeon cote, then dragging them closed again, that no one ever bothered. Outside on the gravel, bumper chromework rusted in the winds carrying salt from the sea.

Originally the building must have been a linhay—linnedge is the local form—when the landholder was allowed to put livestock on to the adjoining pasturage in return for grinding corn for the manor. You can see where newer stones extended it to convert it into a closed barn.

In a spasm of decisiveness I manhandled the doors off their hinges and stored them away. Now people can drive straight inside.

I had an ulterior motive. When I moved to the mill I noticed on the beams in the barn's dim recesses several shallow mud cups: swallows' nests. The passageway had been through a gaping hole at the far end where a side door had rotted off its post.

It had to be got ship-shape. But although I cut hatches in the new door, when the swallows returned next spring they evidently didn't care for the restricted access. They gave their old shelter the go-by.

I missed their rippling blue flight across the lawn, the flash of chestnut throat and white underparts as they soared up from drinking on the wing, their sweet warbling song. Summer didn't seem the same without them around the outbuildings although pairs from the village come racing down the river line which now appears to be garlanded with bunting, the wayfaring trees, the hawthorns, some crab-apples and a big wild cherry all clustered white. The swallows are almost heliotrope against them.

I hoped that, with the main doors removed and that wide portal welcoming them, some renegade swallows would return this year to their old haunts. Some migrants passed through in April; a few lingered and hawked my midges for me along the back leat, but they didn't settle.

I suppose they simply don't like the tinkering with their premises. It seems unreasonably pernickety to me, but you can hardly dictate to swallows where they shall be billetted.

However the alteration didn't go unnoticed by some spry eyes. On the window ledge inside the garage is kept a stone jar of corn for the fantails. The daily scattering feeds not only the pigeons but also a gang of house sparrows, quick to move in on easy pickings.

They not only muscle in on the pigeons on the forecourt. They've now discovered the source of supply. They nip pertly in and perch on the rim of the jar like Eskimos harpooning fish through a hole in the ice. They even plunge inside, belly-deep in mounds of grub. All they have to do is to open their beaks and let it pour in.

Yes, I know—the answer's easy: put a lid on it. Well, I may do, yet it seems a trifle mean to balk that ingenuity. And, who knows, a passing swallow may spot the sparrows flipping in and out, and decide to think again.

*

The three gentlemen from the Council looked worried. I had telephoned asking them to inspect the bridge.

The lane crosses the river just outside my gate. It's little more than a deep rut squeezing between the surrounding precipitous fields. On one side is a low parapet smothered under ivy; on the other, sloe, ash and maple branches plait themselves into a porch where the water narrows into the culvert and provide a moist cave for the spleenworts and wall-rue which have tucked themselves into crannies in the stonework.

The night before I'd noticed with alarm a fissure like the start of a San Francisco earthquake. The road seemed about to fall in halves. Was Wessex crumbling under my feet? Perhaps John ('Everything in the garden's lovely') Maddox, the famous anti-doomwatcher, was wrong—perhaps Planet Earth was caving in under the pressures.

Tracking it back like a Redskin scout through crushed cow parsnip and crowfoot, I detected that a lorry's wheel had swung wide across the verge and broken off a great chunk of the roadway, which now hung precariously on a hinge of crusty tar. Slide area.

Now the Council experts had come to see how to shore it up. But there was a grave and unforeseen complication.

'We shall have to lower the river at the weir to get in the supports', explained the Divisional Surveyor, 'and in the meantime we'll put some chestnut paling and marker-cones around the unsafe part.

'But we're wondering if you'd mind if we delayed the work because otherwise the moorhen will be disturbed.'

The foreman and his assistants nodded in concerned agreement.

Of course—I'd forgotten the moorhen. After being cleaned out by the magpies, for their second go at raising a family the moorhens had shifted location. It was not a judiciously chosen site. They had moved to the most exposed part of the stream and the boobies had built their nest out in the middle on a submerged log. There the hen brooded her eggs without a shred of concealment, within a yard of passing wheels and feet.

There could be no doubt about it: the road repair must wait.

At the weekend from the corner of my eye I espied a stirring under the sitting bird's wing, and a red-dabbed head peeped out. Two days later I saw the hen herding her flotilla of chicks, like powder puffs of sooty fluff, into a cave of undergrowth where the water is still and dark.

The nest was empty. Chicks away. Green light for the great machinery. Operation Landslide could proceed.

And who says that all authority is a bureaucratic monster with red tape instead of human blood in its veins? Moorhens matter—it's official!

*

You did remember Midsummer Day, didn't you—remember that from now on every passing minute is a descent from the meridian nearer to the bitter steppes of winter? I feel duty-bound to pass on that cheerful mid-term message.

I had been up in the humpy field, hammering firm some listing fence stakes. The greensward—upon which theoretically one should be lolling in a daze of scented warmth—had turned my boots to blotting paper. Drooping leaves funnelled rain water down my neck. Frowning clouds scraped the wood.

I eyed with some derision a lowly and inoffensive plant straggling down the bank, the silvery stems of scarlet pimpernel. It's also called poor man's weather glass, because the red petals pout and shut tight if bad weather looms.

Need I say that the scarlet pimpernel was clammed up? I am not easily cast down in the country. But I'll swear that spirits are generally as low as the temperature along hedgerow and streamside. Growth is slow. Even such coarse unstoppables as the docks haven't got far in my hummocky paddock fields, and the thistles aren't high enough to cut (which is okay by me, and I can dishonestly comfort myself with the old advice that if they are scythed before St. John's Day they will sprout threefold).

Insect life is sluggish—I had seen almost nothing of the speckled wood, that yellow-dotted brown butterfly which actually likes wet seasons, wavering about the rank jade grass where the rill runs deep under the weedy hedge. So bedraggled birds have been singing less and working harder to bring home the bacon for their young.

It can't be just middle-aged delusion of sun-scorched arms on school cricket pitches, of timeless hours drugged with the rasp of grasshoppers and yellowhammers' wheezing, of lanes white with dust between massy hawthorns. Surely there once was such a thing as summer?

In the 1670s Thomas Traherne wrote of when 'all time was eternity. The corn was orient and immortal wheat . . . it had stood from everlasting to everlasting'.

Back in my study, drying wet socks while a June wind splattered the panes, I dug out an album of the Shoreham 'Ancients' paintings just to reassure myself.

There were Samuel Palmer's pastorals, and landscapes by Calvert and Richmond and Linnell. Harvest moons were enormous rich balls of butter. Every apple tree had a head on it like a glass of Guinness. Sheep bent at the knees under their weight of wool. From skies of Mediterranean blue the sun irradiated the earth to its marrow.

That's how it was. Or was it?

Perhaps in their good old summer time, Traherne, Palmer and Co. crouched, shivering in these Wessex-standard draughts, expressing their yearning for a heat wave by pretending on paper.

July

Two visitors came striding purposefully across the barnyard. They carried assembled fishing rods, and the whippy tips bobbed restlessly as they approached.

One was dark and stocky, the other fair and slight with eyes as eager as a wren's. Both were about twelve. I recognized them: they were from the village by the castle sconce.

'Sir,' they said in unison, as if presenting me with an illuminated address, 'can we fish your river, please, sir?'

How impressed I was by their good manners and their honesty. I could not help making the comparison with myself at that age: sneaking into a private estate with my greenheart sections slotted down my trouser leg. (Likewise an air rifle, or with egg-collecting tins in my pockets, on marauding expeditions of varied intent.) I didn't ask permission but poached with a calculated slyness concealed beneath tousled innocence.

How straightforward are today's young. These two could easily have crept through the paddock, wriggled through the hedge, and cast their hooks downstream without being spotted.

I didn't go into all that. What a bitter lesson: blessed are the meek for they shall be disinherited in plenteous waters, while the sinful shall fatten on fish. Because what did their honesty get them? Kicked out.

Not quite so brutally. 'I hope you won't think I'm a

spoilsport,' I said, 'but there aren't many trout and I'd rather leave them undisturbed.'

This exchange of courtesies was all very well, but it came to the same thing for them. No fishing. They trudged back up the cart track to their bikes, their step and their rods a bit less springy.

After they had gone I crossed the footbridge and padded softly along the bank to beyond the yew walk. I seldom venture here in summer, simply because it's almost impossible without an Indian tracker and a machete.

The run-wild lupins are smothered by forests of butterbur casting canopies of vast rhubarb leaves, one over another like the layers of petticoats Victorian ladies wore under their layers of over-garments.

A willow warbler, somewhere in the green crevasse, trilled its rising ripple of notes over and over again, tireless as a clockwork bird—soon it will be falling into its midsummer silence, to strike up again a brief coda before departing to the tropics. In a little bay here, below the bridge where the dippers nest, there is usually a trout parked in the lay-by out of the main stream. There it was, a dark gleaming cone—probably a yearling.

My shadow touched the surface. From standstill it accelerated across the gravel at about twenty knots.

I've watched eels corkscrewing into the current. And a friend's son bagged two horse leeches. They pressed their pale suckers to the jam jar like children's noses against a sweetshop window.

But the truth is I don't know what the deeper water holds. Are there pike and perch? Does the slender dace live there and do burly rudd slide through the rushes?

I wish I had let the two anglers see what they came up with. Come back, boys: have a sample on me.

*

The van arrived from Chard—Mr. Hancock with the

fish. Not in finger form, nor cod cutlets. These were live. Lithe, Ferrari-shaped, they skidded around the tank with furious tail-whips.

They were trout, a kind introduced from America ninety years ago. You can see why they're called rainbows. The iridescent magenta streaks glinted as they surged about, forty-three of them in the container.

Their future in Mr. Hancock's possession would have been to surface with brown bread and butter on to a tablecloth. That's why he fattens them at his fish farm. For me they were an indulgence. We slipped them out of buckets into the lower leat.

The rainbow is hardier than our native brown trout (which swim just a few yards away in the stream above this artificial branch which worked the mill) but lives only five years. And my tribe would never perpetuate themselves, for to spawn they must migrate to gravelly rillets. They've acclimatized themselves to breeding in only a dozen British rivers.

These took to the lower leat's deep rushy waters. It's a long pond, really. A strong low current drives through under the house, and spills through the ferns and starwort and mare's-tail over the stone sill of the dam.

I dawdled away hours on the drystone wall watching the dark spectres exploring the cool mysterious grottos and root forests under the flash of dragon-flies. In the evening, as young tawny owls wheezily practised hooting in the beech wood, the leat exploded like bullet-struck glass as the trout leaped to snatch an alderfly or pondskater.

Far from fleeing when they felt the reverberations of human feet on the oak slats of the bridge, they quickly learned that the thuds meant savoury food. I fed them every day with handfuls of smelly granules, and their bodies made long creases in the water as they ripped up the straight, biggest grabs for the winner. Sometimes I dropped in a lump of stale bread and they bopped it about like basketball teams.

How happy a water life it seemed. I had overlooked

another American, a hustler if ever there was. My wife bought a tuft or two of something described in a catalogue as Fairy Moss, 'a small floating fern', an alien called *azolla caroliniana*, which probably stole in on some water-lily roots imported across the Atlantic. This magic pixy dust, one gathered, would charm away that nasty thick weed which grew like wads of cotton wool.

I was mildly surprised at how smartly it got going. It promptly spread down the edges, dappled hems of greens and pinks. Pretty, but pushy. I knew not the half of it. We were away a week. Upon returning I went to take a loving look at my trout. Fetch me a bathyscaphe! The leat was hooded by a coagulated crust of that fairy moss. It had taken on a demonic goblin look.

Panic. Trout need high oxygen concentration. They wither before amounts of carbon dioxide which tench or roach tolerate. All, surely, must have smothered under that hot blanket.

I knotted together enough sheets to escape from Parkhurst. I handed one end to my wife. While I rubbed in her guilt as a reckless sprinkler of Fairy Moss, we repeatedly trawled from end to end, scooping up the dainty scourge until clear water could be seen.

Were we in time? I still don't know. I have since noticed some plops, the flip of a fin. But there don't seem to be forty-three trout in that pond. Tensely I watch for floating bodies.

Meanwhile the *azolla* we couldn't reach lurks lasciviously in the reeds, awaiting its chance to swarm out and capture back the territory wrested from its voracious fairy fronds.

*

I am irreverently against keeping a garden like those in which Kate Greenaway children stand about, spotless and static, among yew bushes neat as pompons and pink roses which have never been trodden by greenfly.

If you want to enjoy a charm, or family flock, of goldfinches sparkling like fireworks on a lacklustre autumn day, then it's worth leaving thistles uncut in a wild corner.

It is best not to be too floriculturally prim and proper. Tangles of brambly undergrowth will attract nesting robins, blackbirds, wrens and warblers. Don't be too fast on the draw with the axe, for by chopping down a mangy hollow stump you could be evicting a tawny owl or treecreeper.

My policy is to let sleeping logs lie. Fallen branches, relaxedly rotting away in the straggle of woodland, provide food and homes for insects, therefore food for birds who feel at home.

This is one balance of payments which can't be faulted. Why go to the cost of killing pests with chemicals when birds will do the job for you—if you refrain from poisoning them?

Well, if you're as sluttish a gardener as I am, you have to find some justification, don't you?

While keeping steadfastly to that creed, I had to admit to myself that the steep bank beside the orchard had got not only out of hand, but probably beyond scythe or flame-thrower. As I fought through on my way back from a walk, I had to face it. It was too tumultuous to be ignored. I stopped averting my head and looked.

In the first Richard Jefferies book I ever had, his *Life of the Fields*, I was caught by his 'dreamy summer haze' —the murmur and rippling of a meadow, 'scented as though a hundred hives of honey had been emptied upon it.'

This unshorn bank of mine looked that luscious. I stepped off the path and slid into the sappy forest. I stretched full length. Thoughts dissolved upward like smoke rings into the boundless blue (diverting around a jet plane's vapour trail) between curtains of feathery green and purple flower-heads of the quaking grass and fescues and bromes.

I was dreamily aware that the torrent of bird-song of only a month ago had become a trickle—a desultory few bars from the cock blackbird which sits on the television aerial like a trapeze artist about to swing through space, the arrogant trumpet break of a diminutive wren perching momentarily on the white skull of a marble bust drowning in a jade sea of cotoneaster which washes over the wall, and the languid recital of a robin.

But the sound is now an overall low drone, the ceaseless soft chit-chat of a chiffchaff and the moaning of a wood pigeon in the spinney flowing into the hum of insects—the great engine of summer life. A bumble bee plopped on to a stem, shook pollen into my hair, then zoomed away along the airliner's trail. It could have been as high as that. The world seen from here was of bee-proportions.

In that same essay Jefferies said he believed that 'ultimately the sunshine and the summer, the flowers and the azure sky, shall become interwoven into man's existence'. Did the flower-children of our time read Jefferies? 'To be beautiful and to be calm, without mental fear, is the ideal of nature,' he wrote. Did the Glastonbury pilgrims know that their slogan had been written a century ago?

*

Within a week the skies had fallen and rain sheeted, all day and all night. The raspberries, loganberries, red currants and strawberries were pre-processed on the stalk into mousse. What a splodge.

Beyond the yew hedge, among the hemlock and butterbur, the multicoloured spires of the lupins are like signposts marking where cultivated flower beds used to chequer-board this wedge between the river forks.

I like it as it is. The chivvying of spade and mower has long been eradicated. Frogs live in the tea-coloured bilge, once an ornamental pond; grass snakes slither through the rank herbage. The stinging nettles are nurseries for red admiral butterflies, and on winter days the thistles flower fleetingly with goldfinches.

On one side, though, is an oblong of vegetable tillage. I'd gone down in search of pickable fruit on the rain-flogged stems. Not much. Anyway, the few strawberries which had survived the battering had a consumer quicker off the mark than I.

A grey squirrel scuttled along a trench, lifted up a corner of the net like a dancer taking a curtain call, and neatly ducked out dribbling strawberry juice. We aren't much plagued with squirrels in this hill land, where only beeches get a secure grip and claw deep enough into the chalk canyons to erect majestic columns; down in the clayey bottoms the sycamores and ash trees are spindly arms waving out of the jungly undergrowth. Although the grey squirrel has a tarnished reputation as a pest—for barking trees and stealing eggs—I don't object to their occasional incursions.

But I do have a different squirrel problem. Three times by three separate individuals (including me) glimpses have been caught of what appeared to be a red squirrel.

Now the rare red squirrel isn't supposed to be in these parts, not nearer than an island reserve on the east of the county. Also I do know that the grey alien from America takes on faint auburn tints in summer.

All the same, I've watched red squirrels in Yorkshire and Scotland, and can recognize that furrier look and rich coppery-gold, and all I can say is that was the impression I had of the poacher which nipped down the catalpa tree by the pool and across the grass to the spinney.

I'm frequently delighted but never surprised by encounters with nature. Our routes are steered by kerbs and road signs; our eyes are mostly directed forward, to a vague mid-distance.

By secret hedgerow corridor, by river, by air-lane, by hilltop causeway, by branch funicular, wild creatures have a million miles of free range, and most of the time we never notice them crossing our path.

Apart from the strawberry-robber, there may be another squirrel roaming about this valley, following the life-lines of the beech mast and fir cones, and the fruit crop now swelling in the hazel thickets of the deep creases in the hills where no one ever goes.

*

Several times a day a peal of hysterical laughter blares across the valley. No, it's not me, reading yet another explanation by a politician of why free democratic speech can be safeguarded only by gagging, muzzling, disciplining, sacking, censoring and preferably also slicing out the tongue of anyone who asks him any questions.

The horse-laugh is actually a bird-laugh. It rings from the beech bluff, or from the riverside sycamores, or from the arthritic apple trees in the tilting field. It bursts out in midair. I see a torpedo shape looping across. It flies as if bouncing along a trampoline. What a buoyant, extrovert life.

Yet really the green woodpecker is quite furtive. I've no idea where this pair nested, although round about are three dead trees apparently bombarded with cannon-balls, the bore-holes to old nesting chambers.

The female just landed fifty feet away. I knew the sex because although both are greenery-yallery with crimson crowns, there is no red on the hen's moustachial stripes. It had come to dig up my lawn with its chisel beak.

It was after ants. It has a snakey tongue, with a sandpaper tip. That's what you need for tucking into ants.

I was tapping at the typewriter on the balcony outside my upper floor office. The woodpecker didn't mind. It interests me why some species—and some individuals—are less hassled than others by people. How perverse or daring or foolish or trusting—or whatever it is—birds can be.

Why did the blackbirds who built in the big magnolia at the front door place their nest beside the bedroom window which is constantly being opened and closed? A blackbird comes to the kitchen for scraps; others tear off shrieking like a burglar alarm at a footstep. One nuthatch wings confidently to the bird table and eats cheese rind—whoever heard of a nuthatch eating mouldy Blue Vinny? One pair of spotted flycatchers camping here built at head height on the house wall. The blue tits which selected a weather-made embrasure in the old crumbling Ham stone of the millroom wall, where the bridge crosses the pond, had about as much privacy as a street news vendor.

Why did the pied wagtails pick a place in the creeper alongside the barn door when there was a Matterhorn of impregnable stone face to lodge in?

As I sat working (and sneaking in some sunbathing, so reconciling would-be hedonism with the reproaches of idleness from the Puritan genes passed down by craggy North Country preachers) two visitors whisked indoors past my ear.

Two swallows. They circled my low-ceilinged office, chattering and banking round the multi-coloured gorges of books and swooped out. They can't still be looking for a nesting place. I only wish they were—all those barns and sheds an open house for them. Just casing the joint, I suppose.

I detest regarding birds as 'tame', as 'pets'. It insults their freedom. But I like to think that the largish number here have mostly absorbed that I am a harmless, if lumpish, hanger-on.

A mystery remains. The moorhens on the upper leat see me as often as any, but they never lose their twitchy shyness.

One audacious robin watched tits on the nut-hopper and now swings upside down to peck out a snack a couple of yards from me (an interesting case of enterprising adaptation) but the bullfinches which nested in the bulky thorns behind a curtain of flushed dog roses and wild honeysuckle hedge flee, a blink of receding blue and white.

Warier than most in winter, a woodpigeon now sits on its second clutch in the juniper brushing my balcony. We occasionally exchange glances, semi-det neighbours. Within sight are a hundred other trees it could have hidden in.

I don't mind at all that it took this one. I merely wonder why. The green woodpecker's cackle seems to be some sort of comment on such pedantic semi-scientific musings.

*

It really has been like living in a minefield. A friend's wife leaped back terrified as I hissed: 'Don't use that door!' She patently thought that the handle was wired up to a booby trap.

I have also seriously considered throwing a temporary blockade across the flagged steps to the lower leat foot-bridge—but then the rainbow trout would be stood up, left hanging about without their daily delivery of alms.

Those spotted flycatchers I mentioned are to blame. We have two pairs again. They've reduced traffic in and out of the house to a tiptoeing, nervous weaving, as if snipers lurked around corners.

One pair commandeered that spot beside the hall window. They built their moss-and-cobweb nest in the worn-out vine which has to wheeze like an elderly uncle blowing up Christmas balloons to extrude a pre-shrivelled leaf. There a bird now sits on speckled eggs, bright eye trained, obvious against that pitted masonry as a diamond on a wrinkled knuckle.

Cheekier still, the other two tucked their nest among the bristles of a scrubbing brush jammed above the kitchen door—if not quite a bed of nails, hardly upholstered. To avoid sending off the birds in a twitter of anxiety, everyone makes enormous detours via X, Y, Z to get from A to B.

Yet what pleasure there is in the presence of these small winged Nijinskys which catch butterflies with dazzling swoops, nosedives, hovers and aerial pirouettes. Summer would not be the same without the flycatchers. When the air is still and the foliage hangs heavy in the afternoons with only a kaleidoscope of shifting coloured patterns of the butterflies upon the buddleias, the garden is made lively with their flashing plumage.

They have a network of look-outs: they lunge from apple bough and land on the bridge rail, from a crumbling stone cherub's licheny head and settle on a poppy stalk—never muffing a catch in mid-flight.

If I have a favourite bird, it is the spotted flycatcher. Its vivacity, its trimness, its sprightliness—it is the very spirit of the light winds scented with May blossom and meadowsweet. And, of course, there's its almost exasperating chumminess with which it deposits itself upon you as a lodger.

A melancholy pang: by this month's end the flycatchers, including the young born on our cottage walls, will begin drifting southward. Then will come the gigantic journey towards winter quarters as distant as Mozambique, as they launch themselves from the Wessex cliffs. Here is the sanctuary of the only pair of peregrine falcons to have made a come-back after the murderous decimation by the uncaring use of pesticide—one pair where once there were eight eyries along those towering miles.

Will the flycatchers evade the hunting peregrines and the hobbys and sparrow-hawks which breed in the intervening oak coombs? Will they win over the unpredictable weather ahead of them?

We human travellers need fortifying with gin-and-tonic and smoked salmon on a plastic tray to help us brave dozing in a supersonic armchair for a few hours.

It never fails to move me that, to be so briefly an element of the English summer garden, the flycatcher drives four thousand miles, through a hundred hazards of storms and food-netters, on those frail three-inch wings.

*

The first thing I do in the morning is peer tensely from the bedroom window to see if the speckled gatecrasher is still around. If you are about to snatch at your bird book to search for the picture of some ultra-rare wanderer from a far-off hemisphere—stay. There is no possibility of confusion with a spotted flycatcher.

My speckled gatecrasher is there, all right, perched as usual on the barn roof. But I view him with neither excitement nor rapture. To be frank, I view him with chagrin for he has thrown me into an ethical tiswas.

He is a domestic pigeon marked like a scruffy rocking horse in splodges of black, white and other indeterminate bilious shades: a flying tartan no clan would own. He looks as if he was knitted together out of dribs and drabs of old rags.

I am not being disparaging about this unfortunate offspring of an ill-matched union, but he presents me with a nagging dilemma.

After a couple of abortive attempts, I got going that colony of fantails in the old dovecote. It had a shaky start.

Now the founding fathers and mothers have fruitfully multiplied. Sixteen birds feed on the lawn and gravel, sun themselves on the guttering, decoratively adorn the roof tops, and take off in sporty Farnborough air-displays of nicely co-ordinated climbs, swoops and rolls across the valley.

They even provide me with an early-warning system for hawks. Often it is a stir of perturbation among them and a huddling down against the tiles which turn my eyes skyward—to descry the dark cross of a high-circling buzzard lazing on lofty winds, or a kestrel patrolling the brow of Round Knoll, no more than a quivering flicker against the heaving contours, and once a hobby speeding on a hunting expedition.

But much of the pigeons' attractiveness is merely pictorial: their immaculate plumage a dazzling white against the sky's blue and the rusty red pantiles of the barns. It won't be much longer.

I foresee, only a mating cry away, those Nordic genes being infiltrated by hybrid spores.

It was a week ago that the freckled loner dropped in. At first it fed timorously, tentatively, at the edge of the flock and perched a little apart. Now he's not only infuriatingly at home—one of the gang—but is revealing his maleness with a swaggering chauvinistic aggression.

At this moment he is, with chest bulging and feathers ruffed, relentlessly pursuing a female round and round the weather vane, with its disturbingly apt phallic emblem of a golden cockerel. She is playing hard to get. But for how much longer?

Self-accusations of racialism, of colour prejudice, of Hitlerian discrimination, of Aryan barbarism circulate in my mind, for I know that to preserve the purity of the stock I should strike down the intruder, dispassionately and with medical precision. I should act now.

But, with such violence on my conscience, how could I again eat at my favourite Pakistani restaurant in Shepherd's Bush, how could I maintain an anti-Powellite argument—how could I look a mulatto London pigeon in the eye?

*

I suppose a balloonist with incurable flying sickness and a miner stricken by claustrophobia could at least swap jobs. But what can be done about a donkey with a buttercup allergy? It's as absurd, in reverse, as Ferdinand drooling over daisies.

Suzy arrived at Christmas, a silvery-white jenny of lively disposition which some describe as playful but which seems to me downright bolshy. Her prettiness was undeniable—slender-legged, with immense long-lashed soulful eyes which rolled beguilingly before she nipped you.

The book said that the well-behaved donkey 'must not graze without permission'. Suzy didn't give a hoot about permission. When being led to the overgrown tennis court she stopped to graze exactly when she wanted to, and stood immovably rock-like.

The book also said that a donkey of breeding and social grace would stand when told to—even lie down so that a mounted infantryman could fire his rifle across its back. Suzy, if the mood took her, ignored the order to stand, and certainly wasn't subjugating herself to becoming a breathing heap of sandbags.

I don't blame her. But I did object to being dragged panting and swearing as she cantered friskily towards the horizon, indifferent to those instructions uttered in the recommended firm and commanding manner.

I'm afraid the buttercups took the wind out of Suzy's heels. In the late spring I went to the paddock to bring her in one wet evening. I noticed her mopey mien. Her head drooped. Her eyes ran. Her nose was sore, and skin was peeling from around her mouth.

No nonsense tonight. Morosely she plodded into the stable and didn't even dive at the pony nuts.

Concerned, I looked up the illness chapter. Good grief, what was there that a donkey couldn't get? Hernias and internal parasites, ticks and bog-itch, colic and colds. It could get grasscrack (a split hoof) and ringworm. It shouldn't be allowed to poison itself by getting within nibbling distance of laburnum, lupins, yew or rhododendrons.

How, I puzzled, had so frail a creature survived? According to the author of my book it has a longer history of domesticity than the horse, and the first Stone Age donkeys may have voluntarily joined the human tribe—to get medically fixed up, seemed likely to me.

But by now poor Suzy's trouble had become apparent. There under the allergy section were described all her symptoms, due to the venomous buttercup to which skewbald and pale donkeys are especially vulnerable.

The advice was followed, the vet called and a shot of antihistamine administered, and Suzy is now less red-nosed and more cheerful—and stroppy—again.

I now watch anxiously for that grasscrack or an outbreak of bog-itch. I can relax about only one additional ailment from which blonde donkeys suffer: sunburn. How thankful I am that that has been one worry less during this damp summer.

Yet a problem remained. Suzy, sore nose apart, was lonely up in the paddock or in the old tennis court, a wired-in oblong of scrub-reversion. She likes company, and when one was busy elsewhere her heart-rending bray, an asthmatic snort of anguish, pierced one's ears and innards.

She was alleged to be in foal when she arrived: she had been running with a jack, we were told. There must have been emotional obstacles of incompatibility; Suzy's promising barrel-shape must have been due to a surfeit of hay or it was a phantom pregnancy. Suzy's neurotic temperament could, I'm sure, manage that. Nothing—certainly not a babe—emerged.

Now she has been away to stud and has, we are assured, been satisfactorily 'covered' by a virile he-donkey. We shall see. Meanwhile the vacuum in her life is being filled—by a herd of heifers.

My farmer neighbour has turned them into my field and, after initial wary amazement at this flood of companionship, Suzy became one of the crowd. She mills about with them, they feed together, they join in spontaneous scampers.

She can be seen, an incongruous ashen featherweight

among the piebald heavyweights, grazing up the hillside. She has become a surrogate cow.

*

I left my valley fasthold and went down the coast to a place I hadn't seen for ages. A changed landscape. An atomic power plant does sort of make itself felt. Also there are now rows of snug bungalows named 'Chatterbrook' and 'Utah'.

But beyond, the lane ran flat into the exposed isolation I remembered. Old woody gorse straggled like fire-trails to an horizon of low moorland hills. Glades of birch and oak frothed purple with rhododendrons.

Spreading to the far harbour was another choppy sea —of heather, bearing sun-bleached logs like wrack.

I recalled sand lizards scuttering as I crunched across on hot days, watching for adders sunning themselves and hearing the clinking calls of stonechats, the harlequin little bird which flirted its tail on sprays of gorse, recalling boyhood nesting forays long ago on the scruffy wastes of Hounslow Heath just beyond the perimeter of Middlesex's new housing estates of the 'Thirties. Now the sky was piled with charcoal clouds: a perfect location for yet another remake of *Wuthering Heights*.

I walked through oases of old oaks riddled with humus-piled holes in which small birch saplings and buckler fern had rooted: strange miniature overhead woods. In turn, the birches in the wet saucers were hosts of a parasitic fungus jutting out from the trunks in fleshy shelves, called the razorstrop because, when dried and leathery, they were used to sharpen old cut-throat razors.

On the saltings ahead, lush with cord grass and sea-lavender, harriers drift through in the autumn; far across on the mud flats were vivid pepperings of oystercatchers, and a cormorant sat on a spar-buoy, its wings arched to dry, like an heraldic emblem.

This is the Arne Peninsula, in the Isle of Purbeck. I wanted to visit it again before its hide is skinned off. Perhaps, too, I might see a Dartford warbler.

I didn't. Yet I would like to think that that dangerously rare bird could have haven here, one of the remaining bits of Britain where it hangs on.

Unfortunately under the heather is something called ball clay. Ball clay is scarce, which is why a powerful mining company is now probing with its test drills. The company is very keen on ball clay. It helps them make an annual £11 million net profit.

You might imagine that Arne would be safe, for it is designated an 'area of outstanding natural beauty' and of 'special scientific interest'. Additionally, there are two government nature research stations and an RSPB reserve.

Silly old us. If a mining company wants to dig it up, then dug up it will be. So I gathered from a flattening chat with a County Council planner, who carefully explained that although he *had* seen newspaper reports about alarm and protest, this did not mean that he was *officially* aware of any alarm and protest.

Furthermore it would require government intervention now to stop excavations. It has, I got the impression, been also designated an area of outstanding potential profits.

Who's Who mentions that Lord Aberconway, chairman of English China Clays, is the Royal Horticultural Society's president. I do so hope he has the chance of getting over the Arne before his machines disembowel it, in time to see the *Erica cilaris*, a downy heather with crimson flowers virtually restricted to this area, among which the Dartford warblers nest.

*

The pressures and intrusions drive not only in upon Arne: they are everywhere mounting; they come close to home.

A funeral has been taking place. On the misty morning the procession started out from the Farmers' Arms in Uploopers and wound past the ducks sunning themselves in the farm entrance dusty ruts, through the ferny mesh of our valley lanes to the limestone uplands.

Six pall-bearers carried the coffin. The wreath was nothing elaborate: speedwell, foxgloves, dog rose, ragged robin—the ordinary wild flowers of the Wessex hedgebanks and meadows. Chaffinches sang in the bushes and a cuckoo made a brief call, a croaky postscript to its two months of talkativeness.

The men wore top hats and frock coats, the women heavy lace veils. There were black ties and armbands, and cars bringing up the rear were draped with crepe garlands.

Those gathered from miles around to pay their last respects were interestingly mixed: the potter and the earl who renounced his peerages, the farm worker and the retired Naval Commander, comprehensive fifth formers and a visiting MP, the young novelist and the schoolmaster, small children and grandmothers.

What were we mourning? The coffin bore two inscriptions: 'Welcome Hill, in an Area of Outstanding Natural Beauty, died owing to lack of protection from greed, stupidity, equivocation and naivety', and 'Here lies an Area of Outstanding Natural Beauty, died of sickness which the Wessex County Council and others did not see fit to prevent'.

Our destination, atop the wild hills below Haggerdown, was marked not only by higgledy-piggledy drystone walls, a wheeling buzzard and what looked like sarsens (were there snouts of glacier which pushed as far south as this?) which you come upon standing like great solitary tombstones, billowed around by brakefern. Jutting above the skyline now are a yellow crane, metal cabins and the girders of a drilling rig—steeple-shaped but erected only in worship of Mammon. Barbed wire and a placard warn off all but the American oil company's team from what was once the local cricket pitch.

At the roadside, beside piles of bulldozed soil, the ex-viscount spoke the last rites in Churchillian resonance, and then the cortège disbanded. We by no means represented unanimous opinion for not marching with us were those who had the sniff of money in their nostrils and perhaps enticing visions of Cadillacs and Texan hats, who like the sound of our slogan 'Oil Means Spoil' for its secondary meaning.

This is landscape sanctified by Act of Parliament as heritage for future generations, protected from industrial invasion. How, then, can the murder of such places be got away with?

Because mining operators smartly respond to invitations to dig up quick profits and don't care where. Because central government—Labour and Tory—flouts the law for a cut in the commercial gain and has encouraged the wrecking of our National Parks. Because local authorities betray the trust vested in them. Because landowners agree to it.

Money talks. Beauty is voiceless. Still we can democratically express our opinions of the desecration of the Thomas Hardy country and its endorsement by the elected officials who could have said no.

So we had our say on the remains of Welcome Hill, but this is Britain's loss, not just ours, and the names of the politicians—professional and amateur—who had a hand in it should be remembered by the larger public they serve.

August

WITH a gambling man's metallic discipline I let several races go by. Before going for broke I coolly gave myself plenty of time judiciously to study form.

In the Fetlock Frolics—sixth circuit of the course—I moved in for the kill. My bet was on Burp (by Spanish, out of Onion). The winner was Ripalong (by Getting, out of Gear).

Easy come, easy go. With a shrug and the twisted bitter-sweet smile which marks the high plunger, I flipped away my 5p slip. However, it had not escaped my notice that Burp, a gunmetal beast bearded along its underparts with a shaggy pelmet, bore an uncanny resemblance to Modern Miss in the earlier PTA Handicap. Moreover it had an extraordinary similarity to a contestant in the Wessex Stakes, Chump Chop.

The proceeds were for the neighbouring village school. One did not, therefore, ask awkward questions about assumed aliases and switched colours. The same six runners (zest noticeably waning) were being reshuffled for the next Donkey Derby event.

Lily the Pink was rummity-tumpting yet again through the loudspeaker. Relay jockeys (limits eight stones and fourteen years) were wriggling into jerseys and swapping hard hats.

Across the broad field rooks went rearing up, a black gunpowder puff from the muzzle of the tractor snorting along the skyline. It was off duty, now towing a trailerful of children on penny rides.

I wandered away from the crowd over to the elegant varnished horsebox parked by the hedge, which was draped, as if for the festivities, with pink-and-white streamers of bindweed. I noticed a ginger cat curled up on a song thrush's nest, and by the cat's air of sleek somnolence I suspected that whatever had been inside the nest was now inside her, a late brood which was too late. On the back of the horsebox there was a notice: 'Donkey Racing Team. Please Pass.' Not very difficult, I thought, glancing back at the grim neck-and-neck struggle being fought out at a sluggish trickle inside the ring of straw bales.

On the van were the stars' portraits, painted on slices of tree trunk. Supernags, one and all. 'Beauty, The Prettiest Marked Donkey in England', 'Snow White, Royal Command Performance', 'Delcia, Christened on TV, Celebrated by Champagne'. What a glamorous lot. I recognized the picture of Beauty. I knew her as Burp. Her real name seemed to me a mite extravagant. About Snow White's and Delcia's honorifics I wasn't quite clear. Still it could hardly be doubted that they had great lustre in donkey society.

How fortunate we were to have them in this quiet corner. These four-legged aces—swigs of bubbly, audiences of crowned heads—were used to the big time. What triumphal grand tours were marked by those placards . . . Skegness, Filey, Barry. No wonder Burp, with her supercilious mien, hadn't seemed to be trying very hard in our rural capers. I couldn't help thinking of Suzy at home in the paddock, with nothing to do but eat and laze. I wondered with treacherous scepticism how she would measure up to the cut of professionalism of these hard-bitten troupers.

Later, long after the skittle alley and the Junior Big Dipper had been dismantled, we were driving home following a pub snack. The headlights touched a vehicle lumbering along the B-road. It was the Donkey Racing Team's mobile home.

Inside, I suppose, were Delcia, Snow White and the rest, bound for the next roar of applause for the *haute école* in some far off gay resort. Between times, there was the truth of the life of stardom: a jawful of hay in the swaying darkness while rain splattered on the wooden roof. Again Suzy came to mind. Hypochondriac though she is, subject to delusions she may be among her bovine chums; but she doesn't realize how lucky she is.

*

He rippled over my shoes like a yellow shammy-leather, a male stoat. I was leaning on the stile. The stream loops under the lane there and ducks into its ivy-curtained tunnel. I felt as placid as the five cows I could see perched on the smooth height of the knap, stiff-legged as tin farm-yard models on a cardboard hill. Everything looked replete and glossy, bursting with abundance. The new molehills in the meadow were like rich Christmas puddings.

Out bustled the stoat from the bracken. He ran across the gateway with a flip of black-tipped tail. His nose slid smoothly as a ball in a pin-table. There was probably the fragrant thread of a rat's track.

It didn't notice the behemoth above it, until I twitched with surprise. It spun round. We stared at each other, about equally startled. He reared on hind legs, lithe as Nureyev in creamy body-stocking, then whisked away into the wood.

The stoat looked in crackerjack trim: sleek with good living but also vibrant with appetite. The chances of any mouse or bird encountered would not, I thought, be conspicuously good.

These are succulent months for predators. The hedge-rows and garden herbaceous borders are thronged with birds tripping over their own Charlie Chaplin feet—youngsters overfed and under-trained, with too few flying hours logged to be sure of dodging to safety.

The juveniles are now just in-betweens, gawky with adolescence. Adult plumage is half on, like children rushing off tò school with rumpled blazers and twisted socks. All the up and coming blackbirds and thrushes and pied wagtails charge about my lawn full of beans—and worms.

The old ones are glum and mopey. All song has stopped. Wasps zizz around their orchard nest. Grasshoppers scrape like toy violins. The birds are silent except for irritable curses at the babies they worked so hard to feed and which now get under their feet.

They are tetchy. They are moulting. Bit by bit, patch by patch, they shed feathers which got worse for wear during the strenuous time of raising families. Nothing stirred along the mill leat except the spurts of dragonflies, the flight of scarlet sympetrum like tracer against the thick fuliginous greenery overhanging the bank. Where were the moorhens? Skulking, I supposed, in their caves in the arrowhead beds and brooklime.

In remote times birds' ancestors probably discarded their outer coverings as a snake wriggles and twists to slough off its skin—the early bird's axis asquirm.

They began to do it in stages. It was playing safe; not so disabling. Some birds start replacing feathers from head to tip; other species strip in the opposite direction, like peeling off a T-shirt. If the clockwork is right, they they are never left wingless or tailless. Alas, the tailoring of the refit isn't always that neat.

As I strolled back to the mill a scruffy dwarf fluttered on to a hazel branch. It was wobbly as a rudderless boat—which it was. The robin had no tail at all. It looked dishevelled and absurd and miserable. You could see it *willing* those new rectrices to get sprouting, fast.

I hoped that in the meantime the stoat didn't spot it pecking about on the ground. I knew which would be the quicker.

*

It's referred to often enough in commercials for all sorts of things in tins and packets and canisters, but no industrial chemist or after-shave lotion manufacturer has yet managed to market it: the scent of new-mown hay.

The air was almost voluptuous with it. I sat on my friend's cottage wall drinking beer brought over from the Horseshoes, and the breeze rising from the slope below could have been blowing with all Arabia's spices, a warm aromatic sweetness.

The tractor—and the old man and the boy—had finished cutting: so late in the year, for there have been few warm breezes to massage the ears to perfect condition, and now it is almost time to reap the wheat and barley. On the far hillside, on bigger holdings, the stubble was scattered with baled yellow cubes like a child's alphabet blocks, prefab components ready for building speedy-rect rural high-rises in the fields. There were several pheasants picking like hens along the verges of the prairie of stubble.

In this patch in front of me a mechanical baler would have had a job making a turn, and the drying swathes, already bleaching blonde, were heaped waiting to be spread to the sun and raked into rows for collection. There was a swaying cliff of uncut wild grasses and flowers, where the wheels had skirted a toft, a plot where a farmhouse had once stood, and whose invisible stone foundations would snap the blades.

This untouched part was rosy with ripe panicles: sorrel, plantain, red clover and white clover, cock's foot, the pinkish spikes of timothy, and heads of fescue like silky yellowish prawns, and all threaded with fire-trails of poppies and the white asterisks of ox-eye daisies. Somewhere down there a grasshopper warbler had been nesting, and during May and June its extraordinary whirring call, like an angler's reel running out fast, and sustained for a couple of minutes at a go, continued through the night. Now the sound was of grasshoppers themselves.

I was supposed to be distributing arts-and-crafts exhibition posters for my wife. Due to an unforeseen important conference with my friend (about the safe flying of the young sparrow-hawks from their gully nest) I hadn't got farther than this first call.

Certain metabolic changes had prevented progress. A sluggishness had crept through my limbs; there was a pronounced paralysis in my torso. A butterfly, a marbled white, basked on a cushion of thyme. It was an effort to turn my head and watch it dancing off into the grass forest like a tatter of patterned wallpaper among the brimstones and meadow browns.

I was far from sure that I could even summon up strength to drain the tankard. I succeeded, and left my head tipped back watching house martins scudding like yachts on a wide blue Solent.

Of course it may have been the additional aroma of hops. I think it was the headiness of high summer which had semi-anaesthetized me, the rich vernal vapours not only of the hay crop, unsprinkled by pesticides and phosphates, but of sun-toasted soil and human sweat—all in conjunction as they should be.

*

The church was fuller than churches usually are nowadays, every pew packed. Hymns were not being sung nor prayers said. There was no sermon.

Instead there was a recital of Renaissance and baroque music. We heard Vivaldi played on lute and harpsichord, some Bach preludes, two Scarlatti sonatas, Boccherini's *Introduction and Fandango*.

Julian, the illustrious guitarist, is a local. He and his wife Margaret got going the idea of this small village festival. In the next parish church during the weekend there was a reading of Thomas Hardy's poetry, here in his 'Vale of Blakemore', close to where Tess was born.

The vicar had had some misgivings. Was church on

Sunday a proper place for the works of a man whose faith had been ousted by a gnawing pessimism about an implacable universe, a rationalist and agnostic who had turned to other sources for a metaphysical system, who wanted not the consolations of an after-life but an 'organic culture' on earth? Poetical values were upheld; the poems were read.

The festival's first night was sultry. It seemed pensively moody. On the way across the Chase, the old royal deer forest, from wide acres of corn stubble rose a legion of lapwings, perhaps two hundred. With a pang one remembered that summer had almost had its run. Already a restlessness was palpitating through the countryside like equinox gales. Bivouacs abandoned: there was a mustering of the pilgrims for the autumn journeying.

Sadness did not set in. At the host's house a lot of us gobbled salmon and swigged Chablis. Off for the concert in a glow of good humour. Heavens, where was some of the sheet music? A furtive, frantic dash from the church to retrieve it from the kitchen dresser.

During the interval, while the light died groups of us drank coffee among the gravestones, with their natural wreaths of daisies and bittersweet, as the first strawdot moths began fluttering to feed in the uncut grass. Again I noticed the flocks. House martins were gathering in the sky for companionship in their coming stupendous odyssey to the south. Their soft sweet song became loud, an aerial chorale as the numbers grew.

Back in St. Leonard's nave, the florid lustre of the Victorian stained glass gradually dulled. No swifts now screeched through the twilight around the spire. Silently they had slipped away, by now beyond our seas. It is the sudden realization of the absence of a thing which can be keenest.

Julian's fingers plucked from the lute the marvellous melodic line of John Dowland's *Melancoly Galliard*. The continuity of the beauty formalized by Dowland four hundred years ago seemed very strong and present there.

In the audience—the congregation—was Anton, the young American who had made the lute just down the lane in the steadings, the derelict cowsheds which Julian had repaired and turned into a workshop. Among us too were Michael and Keith who built the harpsichord which George Malcolm had been playing, and Jose, the Spaniard political refugee who had made the guitar.

Afterward the darkness was shivering with summer lightning. An immense moon radiated a neon glare on the great elms which fasten into the clay-with-flint and the rolling dense woodland which provided the Norman noble households with fresh meat through the winter. There were ninety deer parks in this part of Wessex and the landscape is still grooved with their pales, the earthen banks with parallel wide ditches.

Below the moon hung Venus, a brilliant diamond pendant. It was a bright night for birds navigating by the stars; a clear night for sharing with others the transcendent creative spirit which is Creation.

*

'Watch 'em cock their heads.' On cue two hundred heads cocked. Bob had mimicked a phlegmy *ork-ork*. I myself almost squinted up for a foraging carrion crow.

The juvenile pheasants definitely expected to see one. Eyes scanned the sky. They froze, ready to dart for cover.

A minute earlier Bob had made a different noise. As we threaded through the grass and lofty sunflowers to the wood edge from the tumbledown farmyard where he keeps his stores, and where I often poke around among the haunted nettle-flooded byres and stables, lived in now only by swallows and robins and spiders, he gave a low fluting whistle. Out of the undergrowth the pheasants had galloped, crowding to the fence. Corn up!

Miniature ostriches: hen-sized with gangly knock-kneed legs, plumage still skimpy like shrunken pullovers.

They flap up to roost in low branches. They don't yet venture out of their roofless compound.

It is belted by an electric wire to discourage foxes. The other day one sat on the little green alp which overlooks the preserve, watching the pheasants feeding, poignantly regarding all those unattainable hot dinners.

In the past year Bob shot ninety-nine foxes. That's a terrible one-man toll, yet in these barbican valleys (like trenches dug deep in the sandstone as redoubts for the great fortress of Haggerdown) foxes breed beyond sustenance level. Many of those he killed were stunted and scabby, slug-eaters, scavengers of kestrels' leftovers.

Now how did these pheasants, scooped up as just-hatched chicks so with scant parental discipline, acquire their wariness about the crow gang? Was that recognition a race memory coded into their genes? What is still not imprinted upon them is that the human beings who cosset them with grain, and protect them from crows and foxes, will soon be marshalling their flight across blazing shotguns.

It has taken aeons of development for man to achieve such subtleties of perfidy and paradox. Live for today in your forest glade Welfare State, little pheasants: you will hardly know what's hit you.

But Bob is a younger generation gamekeeper. Although the R.S.P.B. still has to harry those who, illegally as well as ignorantly, exterminate everything with a hooked beak—and unlawfully set pole traps, breakbacks on sawn-off conifers, which hawks like as vantage points, then to dangle upside down with snapped legs held in the steel clutch—they are themselves a dying breed. More now wisely respect the intricate balances and checks which nature, a tough overseer herself, imposes.

Bob told me with pleasure of seeing twenty-four buzzards in one field, that 'hobby-hawks' had nested in the next valley, that sparrow-hawks—gaining ground again after decimation by DDT—from the spruce and larch plantations up at Claw Park hunt his preserves unharmed.

Barn owls bred peaceably in two deserted cottages. Lucky, and ratproofed, is the land-owner with owls on his premises. Why don't the mass-producers of metal agricultural buildings at least design them with nest holes and chambers? In Austria and Germany even newly erected barns have owl holes in the eaves. It is, altruism apart, sound economics.

As we returned to the lane I saw dangling from some brown bones, jammed in a thorn, a jay's blue-blazoned wings. The gamekeeper's gibbet is by no means disused: the persistent egg-robber still gets the chop.

The most recent raider got into Bob's poultry house. There was uproar through the moonlight. Leaping from bed, he rushed, gun in hand, out of the door ready for a rangy vixen.

In a holocaust of blood and feathers, among shrieking hens, was—a hedgehog! End, it must be reported, of the hedgehog with delusions of being a tyger, burning bright.

*

We have just been receiving a new arrival at the mill. She didn't get the cordial welcome deserved by one entering a zone of high hazard.

She is a black-shouldered peahen of glamorous complexion: café-au-lait plumage, shading from creamy-buff breast into a chocolate mantle.

I had supposed that the Indian blue cock would be thrilled. He has been morose of late, dragging about the garden or humped glumly on the balcony rail. He has also been making a fool of himself: tail-fanning and twanging his feathers like a jew's-harp at anything within reach of his breeding display vibrations, a pigeon, a sparrow, even the beagle, who slinks off rolling her eyes uneasily.

The peacock's mate vanished six weeks ago. She had made a maladroit essay at maternity by laying an egg in the stable trough and then forgetting where it was. Later I noticed her furtively prospecting the spinney brushet and weaving through the lattice-work which was once a trimmed beech hedge and is now like a wooden castle. Although we never discovered precisely where she hid herself, I am quite sure that something else did.

Recently the lady at the thatched cottage beside the bridge heard a commotion among the moorhens on her run of the stream. Scampering along the bank came a tawny animal with thick tail which 'brushed out' when confronted. It had, she told me afterward, 'an evil little face'. On other occasions it was seen swimming and nipping across the lane.

It is a mink, which is rather like a big stoat, eighteen inches long and weighing four pounds. Many mink now breed wild in the West of England: the progeny of a defunct Devon fur farm. I knew that they were established in Poorstock Forest's oak swamps, and all around here are mazes of secret clefts choked with rushes and alder thicket, their kind of town.

The mink isn't popular—except, when dead, with girls. But the pelt of the renegade has no value (except to the mink, which is presumably happy wearing it). The mink is branded a bloodthirsty marauder and three hundred were killed in 1971. Now, although they are said to be 'not attractive to hounds' otter packs are after them, since they have almost run out of otters, a situation deeply regretted by the otter-hunters and, conceivably, by the remaining otters.

I wonder if there is need to be so perfervidly anti-mink? I regret that my peahen supplied it with a dinner, which was undoubtedly the case. I thought that she was safe from predators, protected by the streams which moat the place—but of course the mink takes to water like a torpedo boat.

Now an official has been down and beside the river

is a trap baited with dog food. Although the peacock greeted his new companion with truculent pecks, it is, surely, bound to penetrate his tiny thick head how fortunate he is, and hopefully another nest will be made.

I wouldn't want the second peahen to die on duty. Yet I confess that I like the thought of another wild creature being at large and, on the quiet, I'm not sorry that so far the trap has stayed unsprung.

*

The greenhouse would hardly have qualified for a Preservation of Ancient Monuments order, but it seemed to me to be worth saving.

It was a broken skull of a building when we moved in here. Beyond the yew walk empty sockets stared skyward where the glass panes had dropped out of warped and rotting frames; the Heath Robinson machinery for winding open the windows on ratchets was fossilized with rust.

Of course it would have been simpler to knock it down, clear the site and replace it; but I'm not keen on those natty little matchbox-sized metal jobs. The versatile Mr. Lee from Emminster shored and patched up the ruin.

Now it is solid and square-set again and white-painted as greenhouses should be and with ornamental wooden spikes at its gable-ends, and you can walk up and down among the tomato plants and stacks of earthenware plant pots.

Greenhouses bottle summer like Schiaparelli does scent. The heat inside was slumberous; a trapped horse-fly hummed listlessly through the clotted smell of soil and greenery. A prickly pear, ousted from the flower room as dead and done for, and dumped on a shelf, had sprung to life in that torrid corner and was thrusting out tender yellow thorns.

I moved a wooden crate. Curled up where the cave

had been was a slow worm, glimmering like a seam of cinnamon-stone in the mould. I picked it up. It delighted me with the sinuous strength with which it trickled through my fingers, an exquisite form of functional elegance.

Needless to say, the slow worm isn't a worm and nor is it especially slow. Furthermore it is not the snake it resembles, but a lizard which has disencumbered itself of legs. Colin Simms in his book about lizards catches it with scientific and poetic exactitude: '. . . flowing like a molten bronze rod through the herbage'. And he quotes the lines of Basil Bunting from *Briggflatts*:

Ripe wheat is my lodging. I polish
My side on pillars of its transept,
Gleam in its occasional light.

Slow worms hibernate in winter. Down here in Wessex Colin Simms once found eleven all using the same sheet of corrugated iron as shelter—and they weren't even a commune but had drifted in independently. After mating the female harbours the eggs within her body, laying in autumn just as the babies are pushing through the soft shells.

I don't know what my slow worm was up to, lolling about in the greenhouse at this time of the year, with lots of that ripe wheat around, but I did know where it could make itself useful.

Earlier I had been irritably regarding the tatters of young lettuces and thinking: 'Well, if you will be mulish about banning pesticides from the garden, you'll have to take the consequences from the slugs.'

Perhaps not after all. The slow worm is a great muncher of slugs. I transported my captive from the greenhouse to the lettuce patch. Go to it, little legless lizard and feast yourself—I shall be much obliged.

*

Now and then I have twinges of guilt that I may give misleading impressions. I scribble away about a rare bird or a dramatic clash with villainous mining prospectors. The high-light of the week pushes itself forward on to paper.

It is not, here beyond the mighty wall of chalk which boxes us in, a life of concentrated adventure and excitement: this is not the Texas Panhandle of the Wild West Country.

Let me tell you about a far more typical day.

I had been collecting some white willow cuttings from a friend in the next village—probably too early to expect them to take, but they were prunings which might as well be stuck in the soil at a point where I want to thicken the cover on the river bank. Instead of reporting straight back to my desk, I strayed off the straight and narrow Roman road, which streaks inland along the apex of the terrace of chalk. On an impulse I forked right into a valley I often glance at as I buzz by above without stopping.

How did I for so long resist a peeling signpost pointing to De Aquilla Porcorum? Eagle and pigs! Once swine rooted free among the beechmast on a Romano-British family's estate, so it became known as a great place for hogs. Names roundabout are elaborate punning corruptions of Saxon, Celtic and dog Latin, mixed with grand titles.

The Piddles describe the villages where the water dribbles over clay. Down in those muddy snaking lanes the slopes bubble with brooks: winterbourns, the springs which hallmark the dozen surrounding villages, the Winterborne thises and thats.

It took me two hours to get home. I corkscrewed into that wet hollow with its handsome double-depth manor (status symbol of the 1700s, for up to then rooms were built in a row, as at my mill) and the stone eagle perched on its central gable. In the church is a Norman tympanum depicting a stranger creature: two of them, wyverns or winged dragons, with lobster-like bodies and cats' heads, squaring up to fight.

I climbed again to the vast plateau and took tracks out on to top-spurs overlooking my own parish, the outliers like natural demibastions with hornworks of sheer sandstone plunging into slippery blue lias. Like the camera of a spy-plane, I looked down upon unsuspected isolated granges, homecrofts and huddles of barns and skillens. They were scrappy remnants of the hides, or acreage, of 11th-century manorial holdings and their demesne farms.

So puckered and geologically chaotic is this land, that it was only with difficulty that I could pick out and identify these places on my Ordnance Survey map—names so often ending in -hay, or enclosure, whose safety was secured by the inland scarps and massive glacis-like banks. How amazingly little, even today, the motor car has impinged upon, or even infringed, the intactness of these medieval settlements below the Neolithic burial mounds in this Wessex heartland.

I came to a patch I know, through Poorlot. I picked wild strawberries. Along this defile their stems were lacy mats under the nut bushes which dangled clusters among the blackberries ripening in the declining sun of a fading summer. The strawberries glistened bright as coral beads; they had a winy sting on the tongue.

I have my own timetable for taking this particular route: when the trains aren't running. That is no severe limitation, for only six solo coaches a day shuttle between Port Bredy and Chalk Newton on this single track's ten-mile wriggle through lonely, tousselled country. Even this minimal hazard for the adventurous fruit-gathering trespasser will soon disappear: when British Rail lops off this little life-strand for remote, bus-less villages, and thereby pushes more traffic into our tortuous lanes.

I scrambled up to a Victorian brick bridge, once linking farmland but now smothered under buckthorn, spindle and wayfaring trees, where orchids were pale candle flames in the damp gloom.

You must compress yourself (not easy in my case) to a roe deer's lissom lines to thread along their tunnels to the open down. Bursting from the bush, I startled a buzzard hunched on a fence post in ambush for a rabbit, a young bird which flailed gawkily away showing vividly mottled underwing patterns. I had a mind to plunder mushrooms, but instead I squatted ruminatively, staring around from the lofty lookout at the many by-ways and no-ways I have nosed down.

As ever, the gigantic hulk of Haggerdown filled the sky, a green-skinned swordfish lunging to impale Poorstock's shoal of cottages. Gulls oared casually over the old smugglers' passes. A kestrel skimmed down like a ski-lift car to try its luck in the dale lapped by surging bog oaks, the edge of King John's chase.

My eye wandered to the hanging wood where badgers' pads pulp the bluebell stems like grape-treaders, across the brackeny dell where a vixen always cubs, past the barn owls' home in the crumbled lime kiln . . . toward my own village where the mill, and its flash of streams and wagtails, were hidden by the enwrapping ancient land.

To earn the right to love a place you have to learn about it bit by bit. Dear Wessex—'that wondrous world of sap and leaves' of Hardy. He wrote that the beauty and grandeur of a landscape has real meaning only when charged with feeling for those who in the past trod those paths, whose hands planted the trees and ploughed the fields—who, like his Giles Winterborne and Marty South in *The Woodlanders*, looked upon the everyday scene with 'a clear gaze'.

What did I see as the light dulled and I made my way back to more beaten tracks? Nothing remarkable, just immense space and quietness. Gorse spitting yellow sparks. Rooks blowing like charred scraps across great fields. The sun threw up thin white arms as it drowned in cloud. Bullfinches shot ahead down the hedge. A pheasant crossed the road, neck thrust forward from white collar like an overworked curate on his rounds.

The light had become peculiar, mysterious. The land form dissolved and solidified again in a ruddy haze, and wind-crippled thorns with knobbly joints seemed to move like Ents, Tolkien's tree spirits, through the opalescent mist. And when, as I descended the ridge, I came upon a human being, an old man in a brown overcoat shuffling up a woody lane, at first I thought, in a pulse of fright, that he was a wayside oak—advancing on roots!

I was feeling vaguely uneasy on the exposed heights, in such solitude, with darkness lapping against the Iron Age camps and the beacon peak. Four miles across the gap Haggerdown looked as unsubstantial as a dream hill never to be reached.

I hurried back to the clattering warmth of the house, where dinner was cooking and the windows shone.

Absolutely nothing had happened.

September

THE wasp man cometh—I was relieved to hear this from the nice Council chap on the telephone. Strictly, he confided, wasps aren't within the Pest Control's theatre of war.

Rats, mice, bedbugs—fair enough: they're all-in on the rates. But (he gave me clearly to understand) wasps are not officially listed for search-and-destroy ops. Still, their officer could probably help. I felt his wink vibrate down the line.

The officer was but a boy, an upstanding, up-and-coming exterminator with a rural Beatles hair-do. Down in our part of Wessex there are still young men who don't train as computer mechanics or hunger to read sociology at Essex University. They follow their fathers and become shepherds and thatchers—and rodent operatives.

He got a warm welcome. The wasp colony in my garden seemed to have multiplied into a system of nation states. A teeming wasp megalopolis, the biggest of them, was situated down a disused mole tunnel in the vegetable patch (really an underveloped asparagus bed in a sordid state of unkemptness). I suspected that it was from here that most of them came into the house, far too many for comfort. They lumbered about the kitchen dull-wittedly, impervious to the brush-off. The wasp is not as fly as the fly.

I didn't care that they were sorting out the ripe pears and plums on the espalier branches against the hot stone wall, where the sunlight gathers almost viscously, but they were now gatecrashing in unswattable hordes, into private meals. I had not interfered while they kept to their own territory. In fact I had sat on the drystone wall and watched them droning through the late summer sun with cargoes of wood, shreds sawn from trees with their mandibles for pulping: a miniature industry producing newsprint for the immediate, instead of second-stage, use of keeping themselves warm with it. The wasp builds its palace of paper.

I saw that, a bit unhappily, when the young wasp-destroyer inspected the entrance, like rush hour at a Piccadilly Line subway with two-way bustle. The grass was black where I had ineffectually poured diesel oil down. Since then the wasps had seemed sleeker and faster on the higher octane.

''Tis a rare year for wasps,' said the Officer. 'Been rootin' 'em out like spuds. One lady had a hornets' nest like a rugby football in her shed. She wanted to keep it there.'

That was how I felt about my wasps when the fearless wiper-out of wasps flicked down some cyanide powder, then heaved out the nest with his spade.

It was beautiful. It was a fragile pineapple, constructed in layers. Each was perfectly architectured, a network of delicate diamond-shaped chambers (four hundred in each storey: I counted); in her apartment house made of wallpaper, the queen had laid an egg in every cell, the cradle for the grub.

The microcosmic world had the symmetry of an atom—or of the universe.

It nagged at me. Had I the right to smash the wasps' city to protect my marmalade jar? The pest controller reassured me: 'That one nest would've produced thirty thousand young,' he said. One nest of one of Britain's 290 different kinds of wasp!

I would have been ready to settle for peaceful

co-existence. Yet that thirty thousand could have tipped the balance of power decisively.

Dead are the wasps; their nest is powder. But the garden is quieter.

*

When I moved to the mill house a dried-up ditch stretched from under the mill room three hundred feet to the yew hedge and vanished into a yawning pipe which re-emerges in a damp little dell. Once water from the upper leat had pushed around the huge wheel, foamed out the other side and filled this small canyon, but the holding wall had disintegrated.

It was fifty years since the mill had ground corn for the village. The wheel had gone; the three worn grinding stones were scattered in the garden. Later the stream had driven a generator and had continued surging on through the house tunnel until mains electricity came. The turbine still bulges in the mill room, rusty and cobwebbed, a fossilized mechanical brontosaurus, and the input and output had ceased.

In those early days here I had peered with dissatisfaction into the ravine. Things weren't as they should be. Below the steep banks, shaggy as a pop musician's brow with rank stems and ferns, there was a cocoa-coloured ooze in a bed of grey clay.

It would be good, I thought, to bring that rancid little wadi back to life. With yellow rock from the hillside I built a dam, five feet high, slotted deep into the banks and crowned with heavy Portland slabs found in a builder's yard in the market town. Slowly, almost imperceptibly, the water climbed up the banks and up to the top of the dam and then began spilling over, a gentle waterfall. Nettles and scrawny elderberries were drowned. A long, broad pond shone in the sun rays.

A week later as I crossed the lawn on the way to fetch vegetables a glint of colour caught my eye, a tiny flash of turquoise lightning against the dull sky. A dragon-fly. A big one, an emperor by the size of that body like a lacquered crochet needle and the splayed golden wings. It was laying eggs in the new lake. It soared high, then swooped and, hovering, thrust its ovipositor against stems floating up from submerged plants.

Around here they call the dragon-fly the 'horse-fly'; I never quite narrowed it down to what they call the horse-fly. Never mind, fly of the dragon, or horse—or unicorn—I was thrilled to see it. The pond was acquiring the inhabitants a pond needs.

Three months after that swallows were skimming the surface, hoovering up midges. At twilight I saw a pipistrelle bat, remarkably like Batman, take a drink on the wing. The surface began to spangle and wrinkle as may-flies and demoiselles and water boatmen plopped and scurried.

Then I saw yet a different pattern on the surface: a vigorous V materializing from bank to bank. It was being made by the long droopy snout of a water shrew, which was chugging, well, nosily, through the new territory. It looked in profile like Barbra Streisand at Miami Beach.

And only an hour later zipping away from an over-hanging ash bough went a metallic arrowhead bigger and brighter than the dragon-flies. It left a reedy whistle in the air like a contrail. The kingfisher had been overprompt on the scene: it was too soon to find much to dive for.

It did before long, for now the millpond has been colonized by rushes and meadowsweet, and the rosy clusters of codlins and cream, and up from a scoop with a jam jar came a creature which, magnified a million times, would be much more dragonish than a dragon-fly. In every detail it was a monster from a Jurassic landscape, lemon body and a warty black back with a ruffle of scales undulating down to its rubbery tail: a great crested newt.

So much of the time we are driving nature out. When it is let back in, how readily—forgivingly—it repopulates and enriches.

*

At this time of the year I can just about cope with the oceanic swell of plant growth, wanted and unwanted (i.e., flowers and weeds) as far as the five-barred gate.

In the field beyond the gate, which climbs steeply to a batch, or hillock, is the remnant of an orchard, wizened geriatric trees on which lichen hangs in grey billy goat's beards. It is in this double paddock that Suzy spends most of her time.

At the centre is a boggy hollow which in spring is smeared a thick yellow with marsh marigolds, like melted butter. Grass rises powerfully in the field, but it is not that faintly shimmering rainbow of many clovers and sorrels and plantains, but rather leathery grass which coarsens into sedge. It is not bad as rough fodder and the farmer whose land adjoins finds it a useful extra stretch when beasts are fattening.

It is a satisfactory arrangement: he pays a peppercorn rent; his cattle get a good feed; and the field is chewed down smooth and sweet for me. All I had to do was lop back a couple of wild-grown laburnums (poison for cows) and jam a branch across the gate as an extra bar.

This lot of Friesian heifers are bouncy and playful. They crowd up to you, jostling each other to get a good close-up stare, and they gallop about, with Suzy usually leading the charge, in romping games.

I can look into the field from my window over the mill stream. I saw a fox come mooching down the hill, bedraggled in the fine rain. Was it the one who got my second peahen, I wondered, scowling at it: a scattering of pale brunet feathers had been discovered at the top of the paddock where the beech roots bulge like knuckles from the sandy bank—and where holes vanish into the darkness of underground lairs. I was pretty sick of laying on expensive banquets of plump peahens for uninvited guests. I scowled harder at the fox.

The heifers spotted it. Sport. They flicked their tails and clumped merrily over. The fox paused, flattened its ears and backed off from the closing ring. The heifers followed. The fox snarled, looked at those thudding hooves, and, turning, went back the way it had come at a smart lick.

Apart from acting watch-dog (where were the real dogs, anyway? What was going on around here?) the heifers solved another problem for me.

Over the back leat, when I was sure that the dam was holding and that the pond would stay put, I had built a wooden bridge. At first the newly-cut stone and cement filling of the buttresses stood out raw against the weathered three-foot-thick walls of the house.

Still, I said to Tom who built them, I supposed moss and lichens would eventually take hold. 'Well, now, that's easy done,' said Tom, looking secretive. 'I'll tell ee, if t'were me I'd follow them young beasts in the field and bring back a bucketful and give that stone a good coating. Nothing so nutritious.'

Did I think twice about this horticultural adventure? Yes, I did.

Having thought, I staunchly went forth among the healthy heifers with a bucket and shovel. I returned and plied the stonework lavishly with a paint brush unlikely to be wanted for any interior Georgian friezes.

It glistened. It dried to a tawny stain. Then it began to be spotted by the spores of little lowly plants, and the sprays of a wall-rue—one of the tiniest forms—uncoiled from a crevice.

Green grow the mosses, O! And the buttresses look a hundred years old with their instant antique finish.

*

When I first came to live in this part I was asked occasionally up in the pubs at Poorstock and Nettle if I'd yet bumped into the phantom stag. Guffaws.

I gathered that the wraith with horns on top was oftenest seen just after closing time. That was when a chap might be homeward bound from the Marquis or the Horseshoes (spirits thick in the air) along the trackways winding around Haggerdown.

The country which falls away from the mighty prow and its spurs and touts, and then lurches into more diminutive ranges among the heath and oak swamp to the down scarp beyond Chalk Newton, is the most desolate in the South-West. Even in summer grey mists like muslin fold wetly upon it.

If ghosts gravitate—or levitate—toward solitude they would feel at peace here.

Haggerdown itself, the bleak spine of rock and the ramparts of the Stone Age fortress, is steeped in ancientness. 'As old as Haggerdown Hill' is a local saying. They also tell of a farm boy, unwisely taking the top path after dark, who met the Devil up there. He ran so hard that the sparks spitting from his boots left a singed trail down to Poorstock.

Another animal of pale complexion (I mean the white stag not the farm boy) is the white rabbit which is said to lope into Poorstock to presage a death.

But the spiked shape seen on Haggerdown's slopes was no apparition. The deer was alive and lusty: a big fallow buck which roved widely through the mizmaze of valleys, like bracken-curtained tunnels, and gathered at the autumn rutting ground on the common to battle—or at least make hostile gestures, for much of this roaring aggression is make-believe—with other males.

The fallow is the biggest deer in Wessex but the sika, a Japanese variety which swam ashore from a private zoo on a harbour island and spread along the mainland, is almost as brawny. They live with the roe deer (re-introduced to the county at Middleton Abbey in the

19th century and now widely distributed) in the Forestry Commission young timber and scrubby coombs, where there is also another escapee, the tiny muntjac, about the size of a spaniel.

They are stealthy. You see little of them . . . A flash and a swish in the sea-green glades of Claw Park. A group like smoke at a copse edge in winter twilight. A dappled russet gliding between shadow and sunlight in a rhododendron grove.

There are more than reveal themselves. The last census suggested that there are 1,200 head of roe, 450 sika and a hundred fallow ranging the Commission's 14,000 acres—but they are just the ones on the official register. The unestimated numbers in bramble under-cliffs and neglected woods are anybody's guess. Spongy paths are pockmarked by their hooves. Their barks and squeals sound at owl time. And evidence of their presence is the crop damage, trees stripped by nibbling and frayed by antlers as territory blazes and to rub off fur from new antler points.

So they are shot. The culls are to keep numbers down to a couple of thousand. But the thinning isn't done only with high velocity rifles in marksmen's hands firing fragmentation bullets. Shot guns randomly spray the woods in poaching expeditions and the haunches end up at the market in the seaport and in local snackbars where venison sausages are served up.

Thus went the white fallow buck. It was seen limping, then a week later hobbling—and killed in mercy. A front leg had been almost severed by a poacher's .22 bullet, a gangrenous wound.

'How could anyone have fired at him?' said Bob, who is a gamekeeper and not sentimental. 'But he had two does. He may've left his mark. There may be a young white buck born.'

*

On the wilder side of the garden, where the beech hedge mixes with the wind-sown ash and spindle and sallow which cascade down the river bank, there is now a flat rock in the long moist grass. It has the look of a small gravestone. It wasn't put there for that reason, but in fact that is what it is.

I mentioned earlier how the Wessex air, pungent with the smell of badger and fox and rabbit, had galvanized my over-domesticated dachshunds—likewise the beagle, Galadriel, named (with ever more evident absurdity as her portliness increases) after the fairy queen in *Lord of the Rings*.

The trio began going AWOL on extended hunting forays. Mostly it was to the woods that they went and, as their earth-plastered coats showed, down into deep burrows, but they weren't always in pursuit of game. A nearby farmer's wife telephoned to ask—with admirable mildness—if we'd mind fetching our dogs, from whose jaws were being prised the dead hens. She demurred at being paid the value of the dead birds and had to be persuaded to accept the compensation. You can tell how good-hearted and understanding are my neighbours, but tolerance has its terminal point and I could not see how to be sure that another raid would not be committed.

I sentenced them to terms of being tethered. I raised my voice to a pitch where I frightened myself. I blocked every obvious bolt-hole, but with boundaries of shallow river and labyrinthine thicket there was no containing them. I shut them up in the old tennis court: a reasonable habitat for any but the most spoiled dogs, but you would have thought from their tremulous moans that they had been locked in a coal bunker.

After a lull, when I foolishly began to believe that they had reformed, they sneaked away again. They were missing two nights. Tilly, the dach bitch, and Gally turned up, exhausted and subdued. It was afternoon before we heard about Duffy, Tilly's four-year-old son.

His body had been found on a B-road three miles

over the hill. There was no blood, no mutilation, so presumably it was only a glancing blow from a passing car, but it had killed him.

Duffy had unattractive traits. He was inclined to slyness. Under a disguise of innocence, he slunk. He was the one repeatedly to be discovered curled up in an armchair or the big saggy sofa in the sitting room, to which he tiptoed. Also, as became clear, he was the ringleader on those break-outs.

For since his death the other two do not go beyond the surrounding fields. Although some may scoff at such anthropomorphizing, it is not enough to say that they miss him: they mourn him.

They were good companions with an intricate three-direction relationship, and the sawn-off Duffy and the large, lolloping Gally, under whose belly he could walk without ducking, loved each other in male and female way.

With him gone, Gally and Tilly have changed. All these months later, their dejection makes his absence still tangible. They know where he is. We found them digging where we had buried him, so the stone was placed upon his grave.

We have also planted a rose there. Sentimental? I don't think so, for a family irrevocably alters when a member is lost, and it is well to keep remembrance. The flowers will feed upon his minerals and be brighter.

*

How do you give a hedgehog the kiss of life? I shrank from the call to heroism. Unhappily I took stock of that sharp snout under its helmet of spikes. Little piggy eyes were closed. Only a tremble of whiskers, a faint shudder in its thistly belly, revealed that life still ticked under that armour-plating.

It was waterlogged. My son had come into the kitchen looking baffled. 'It isn't easy,' he announced, 'giving a hedgehog artificial respiration. It's like kneading a gorse bush.'

He had gone to scoop leaves off the swimming pool. There it was, floating like a mine awaiting a ship to blow up. It saddened me. That pool continues to take an almost unacceptable toll of shrews and wood mice and other small night-time wanderers which topple in and then can't pull themselves out.

It is not that hedgehogs cannot swim: they can and do, without grudge or grumble. But having tipped off the coping during darkness, this one must have exhausted itself clawing with its stubby legs at the high smooth sides. Motionless, with legs now spreadeagled, it had looked very drowned.

Yet when hauled out it feebly attempted to curl into the usual defensive shape of a conker shell. Now it was stretched on its side. The family stood gazing down, mourners at a death bed. How strangely prehistoric it looked, a midget coryphodon under the massive carapace, its quills no longer martially pronged as Shakespeare's 'fretful porpentine.'

Action was needed. It must be dried out, like a drunk picked from a skidrow gutter. A grocery carton was lined with newspaper. The near-corpse was gingerly lifted inside. It was borne, as though in a coffin, into the scullery and put on an airing cupboard shelf with a saucer of warm milk near its nose.

I didn't expect it to survive. Soon the fleas would desert their sunken ship and make for the piles of freshly ironed clothes. Do not be censorious about the hedgehog's lousiness. Imagine being neckless and trying to dislodge parasites from ten thousand horny spines. You would shrug philosophically and likewise learn to live with fleas.

Later a scuffling and scratching caught my ear as I was carrying dishes to the sink. I opened the cupboard door upon a gust of hot air. Revived, the hedgehog was trying a jailbreak. It looked as lively as any hedgehog can hope to look.

I took the box outside on to the lawn and turned it on its side. At a top two m.p.h. the convalescent shuffled out and paused uncertainly for a second. Hedgehogs have poor sight, so rely mostly on hearing and smell. With nose at carpet-sweeper level, he moved toward the shrubbery behind the yew hedge.

He seemed to have picked up the scent of familiar ground, his hunting range for young voles and toads and spiders. I stood in the twilight and listened to him snuffling and crashing through the sun-withered stems and the first sprinkle of autumn leaves: there was a reassuring firmness about the step.

There was a time when it seemed that the hedgehog would be exterminated by the car, for its instinct to roll up and fan out its prickles didn't even puncture a tyre. Now scientists are noting a new tendency toward evasive action. There may be a new strain of run-for-it hedgehogs developing—because they are the ones left to breed and, possibly, hand down acquired tactics against the killer car. It's too much to hope that counter-action against swimming pool risks are also being incorporated in the hedgehog's double-helix.

I hoped at least that this one had now got the scent of the pool firmly lodged in his sensory warning system as a no-go area. I know that hedgehogs eat snails. Surely he cannot have some aberrant fixation about water snails?

October

'WERE you at that meeting', remarked the parish councillor, 'when the Ladies' Keep Fit Club were at the other end of the room? Quite distracting.'

'No, I wasn't at that one,' replied the second parish councillor, looking thoughtfully, perhaps regretfully, deep into his ham salad.

As you can judge, much goes on in the village hut. At the Harvest Supper the ham was followed by trifle and cheese. Jugs of beer and cider circulated alertly.

The farmers' wives served those who had brought in the harvest. Well, I did pick some apples. After I had placed seven million on the storage trays in the dim little shed beside the stables, the boughs still creaked with their rubicund burden. I refused the cider. Beer for me.

The curtains juddered back for the concert. (The cord lasted almost to the end before snapping.) The benches had been pulled round and everyone settled comfortably for the entertainment. The Poorstock Women's Institute did a comedy-drama; the Melton members performed a dramatic comedy.

Massey-Ferguson tractors would not drag from me which was the better. I was visiting Poorstock; I live in Melton.

Auntie Isabel, who is eighty-five and milks her own cows, whispered that 'Shep' wouldn't be doing his turn as he had moved away to start in a new job. After fifty years here he has gone to tend sheep on distant hills, three miles away.

So we didn't hear his old Wessex songs: of such colourfulness, I am given to understand, that, if put on television, they would be indicted by the National Viewers' Association as the poisonous effluence of fashionable permissiveness.

Instead we enjoyed a local guitarist in pink velvet loons singing about a New Orleans brothel called the *House of the Rising Sun*. We know what's going on beyond Casterbridge and Piddletrenthide.

For instance, John's wife this summer had her first holiday since marrying thirty-seven years ago. She went by coach to Rome. She was struck by the Italians' farming ideas. But I doubt that we shall see vineyards on neighbouring slopes which are still terraced with strip lynchets, where once grew flax for the Port Bredy rope-makers. They made cord and spun twine in the villages, too: a century ago labourers' wives earned a few shillings a week extra at this, and many of the mills—perhaps mine—put in new machinery for spinning tow and hemp.

The comic was wearing the standard comic's uniform —from that period. He was in smock, red kerchief and had straw sticking from under his battered hat. But in broadest Wessex he told jokes about Pakistanis and about a man with multi-hued children whose wife was swallowing Smarties instead of the Pill. Every joke was carefully cued from a piece of paper he took from his pocket and consulted, then replaced, before launching into the next roof-raiser.

Finally there was a sing-song and a conga.

Times, you see, have changed. There aren't now the numbers of field labourers who came to these suppers in the past. Today baling machines and combines gnaw swiftly through the ripe stalks. On one local farm even ploughing is being dispensed with. The old natural grasses on high and 'difficult' land (therefore where the ancient sward and its butterfly and ecological chain had up to now survived) are being destroyed with a chemical spray so lethal that it irrevocably finishes off any human being who mistakenly drinks it (as have about a hundred, now dead, throughout Britain). Then the desired ley mixture seeds are drilled straight into the earth, and heavy doses of nitrogen follow.

On the Roman road over the downs there's a stack with a new thatched top, a rare and pleasing sight when straw cubes slot easily under metal skyscrapers. The new technology, the deep freezes and fast transport for food, have taken the fear out of the stark stretch of winter. Of course that is good—but I wish I could feel sure that the methods of achieving that are wise.

Yet in the parish hut there was a sense of long continuity and communion with others who had gathered to celebrate a year's work done, in thanksgiving for the safely garnered fruits. It still matters—harvest home.

*

It had rained earlier. The sun blinked open, bloodshot as a hungover eye, across blankets of woolly cloud. Its bleary stare winced at the brilliance of my boundary hedge, crimson with haws, purple with blackthorn fruit. Rusty grasses steamed. The air was beery with autumn smells.

I thought I would visit my local Brazil. Up the lane starts a Forestry Commission tract. On the skyline is the wild sprawl of Haggerdown. Between there and here the Commission has filled a shelving vale of heath with conifers.

Some people hate the Commission. I wish they didn't have that shed at the entrance gate stacked with cans of Kilbest herbicide, which wipes out scrub—and also butterflies. Much of their early landscape infilling with solid phalanxes of conifers, slung like saddles across clean lines of mountain country and downs, was disastrous brutalism. There is greater sensitivity now, and broad-leaved deciduous belts break up the quick cash-crop telegraph poles.

Nevertheless I prefer the natural self-regenerative patches of what the Commission dismissively calls 'scrub-oak'. For these straggles of squat, gnarled trees in saucers of squelchy peat among sedges and sphagnum, and laced with dense thickets of hazel and flushes of mature alder and thornbrake, pulsate with life. Where the 'oak-scrub' grows more matted in the humid, shadowy wet hollows of Poorstock Forest (which defeated generations of timber-gatherers, huntsmen and charcoal-burners) the scenery cannot now look much different than it did to the early Britons, protected by the linear earthwork defence system of the Great Dyke, and then by their own wooded marshlands, from the Saxon invaders.

Still, even where the Commission has chewed into this older landscape, I don't find their plantations dull and lifeless—the usual complaints. I like their deep green mystery. You thought I was exaggerating, mentioning Brazil? Wait until I tell you more about this jungly place.

I took a favourite sandy ride, where woodcock and nightjars fly in summer dusks. Then I turned into the wood, along a stream bed which gurgled with water stained like tannic and falling fast down the steep rough ground. I scrambled up into the Amazonian interior. Between the black trunks the light filtered opaquely as if through the thick glass of a gin bottle, a dark swimming green. Dying foxgloves drooped into the stream, sedges tufted banks which had velvet collars of moss.

Now what kind of moss? I remembered that Britain has six hundred different mosses—a scrap of knowledge like that makes me feel terribly inadequate, a babe in the wood. I shall die and never know my mosses.

A rustle. A deer? In the paste of mud were the sharp, wedge prints of one which had drunk at this dark pool. Or a mink? They live renegade in the boggy thickets and

I have found their splodgy tracks, with separate lobes, along this stream.

In a clearing a hen sparrow-hawk had died, but how it was impossible to know. Its wings, short and stubby but bigger than the male's identified it as a female. The rest had been munched down to the rufous feathers by a fox, which had then left droppings as its signature.

Upward into the damp tangled gloom, veiled like a Victorian drawing room with vast fronds of fern. But dull? Look at this exotic crop under the warmish drizzle.

All around fungi bloomed, too vivid and reptile-slimy and sickly sweet for our sensible brisk countryside. They shone, livid and doughy in the half light, on decayed leaves and spongy logs.

I am better at fungi than at mosses. I could put names to those waxy orange trumpets and cold mauve parasols, enchanted names of saffron milk cap and chantrelle and tawny grisette. And beside a birch stump, which was soft and clammy with rot, was a cluster like round cakes in red sugar icing stuck with shavings of desiccated coconut: the kind in Beatrix Potter and in Disney cartoons.

But the fly agaric isn't for the nursery. It is a magic mushroom, partially poisonous too. A nibble produces a private *Fantasia*: delirium, hallucinations.

I circled the delusive bright buttons, and then headed out of the haunted pagan forest of dream and mythology. That wasn't what the Commission intended when they started a nice little busy turnover in chipboard and fence stakes.

*

As the sun westers beyond the tail-end of the chalk seam and the light curdles to lavender in our valley, there comes from the tree on the lawn the sound of eventide.

KRRRRRRRRRK - AKAKAKAKAKAKAK - ZGGREEEEEEEET!

The guineafowl are announcing that they are back for the night. There is a Brand's Hatch screech of paws on scorched gravel. The beagle skids round the kitchen corner, followed by the dach pounding slit-eyed through her dust.

They hurl themselves at the lime. The beagle bellows in an anguish of blood lust and frustration. The dach's yelp is sustained at a piercing crest occasionally reached by the late Louis Armstrong.

Safe on their roosting bough, the guineafowl lean over and jeer at the dogs. They drown the baying and yapping with their shattering raucous blast, like metal curtain rods furiously rattled inside empty oil drums.

It is a well-known fact that the countryside is peaceful. Guineafowl cannot grasp this. They are noisy, quarrelsome foreigners who have not fallen into our seemly, staid ways. Possibly they appear more fitting in their indigenous habitat of the African continent, where they live like large pheasants—indeed, that is the kind of bird they are—in the bush and savanna veld. I wish they had stayed there.

I have been called a bird-lover. I can also be a bird-hater. The guineafowl did not win my affection, even though they were an inheritance. They came with the house—feathered furniture and fittings.

The previous owner could not catch them to take with her. Did she really want to take them? The guineafowl are too habit-bound and peabrained to try a new life elsewhere, where they might feel warmer vibrations than radiate to them here, where they might be pampered with heaps of food.

From the start I suspected that we would not get on. When I first walked round the mill and its grounds on a blackening winter afternoon, I came face to face with the four guineafowl. They crouched on the flint wall beside the barn and scrutinized the newcomer with malevolent glares, and then proceeded to screech abuse.

Guineafowl are not dolly birds. They have vulturish

bald heads and stringy necks jutting from absurd beachball bodies. All right, gang, I thought spitefully, if that's your attitude, no more handouts—fend for yourselves.

Fend they have, and farther afield. They have become the Wild Bunch of Wessex. Sometimes when I am driving to the market town to post a letter I see them at the laneside.

They crouch in the hedge like highwaymen, and I hear their tommygun rat-a-tat-tat spraying me as I accelerate past.

But each evening they flap down from the hilltop where the lane runs and return to the garden to show whose turf it is, bovver birds—your actual skinheads, too—bent on a bit of aggro. Wherever I am in the house their earsplitting catcalls rake me. Out roar the dogs, and the shouting match is on again for another half-hour.

It is theatrical provocation. If opportunists like Konrad Lorenz and Desmond Morris hadn't nipped in ahead, I could write several books about territorial protest demonstrations.

I eye the twelve-bore on its rack, kept for rats and oil prospectors, but I do not, in the end, turn it on my persecutors. I am restrained by the thought that they were here before I was. Perhaps they have the right to be here to pick my bleached bones clean.

*

After the hot stony place whence I winged to snatch a brief holiday, returning to England was like stepping ankle-deep in lawn-cuttings: soggy, dank, green, soft, and heavy with a sweetly rank smell. Back in these valleys, like a giant's axe blows chipping wedges out, there is now a clogging of rusty leaves and vapours hang above them, trapping the dew and rich scents. I breathed it all in deeply after being scoured by dry winds.

But what I want to exhale upon you from these river

everglades is a breath of stale air. The moment I walked into my work room after my absence I realized that it cannot be ignored. I had obviously been chloroformed by custom, but approaching after an interval it is without dispute a feted place.

Given the merest flash of sunshine I can shift my typewriter on to a balcony where a woody old rose entwines through an ornamental cast-iron railing. With perhaps a buzzard thermalling over the Knoll's conical hump or wagtails like lean-hulled competition craft on the millpond, jibbering the kibber with flickers of yellow, I can bird-watch while writing.

Inside it is I who am watched. Balcony door closed and desk lamp on—then my every move is observed by ten pairs of bright black eyes. Perhaps I am being hypersensitive, even neurotic, about being under constant surveillance. I feel like a Guy in a White Hat stalking up to the bar in a Western saloon filled with Guys in Black Hats, the small of my back crawling with a concentration of gazes. Also I feel like Winston Smith huddled in his gimcrack flatlet under the relentless scrutiny of Big Brother's telesnoop. Is there no hiding place?

Not that this mass observation is malevolent. No, it is amiable and eager, as is the nature of gerbils. I never intended to have ten gerbils camping in four stacked cages. They all stemmed from a pair brought home by my daughter—temporary digs for them while she found temporary digs for herself, but now, it seems, their permanent residence. Now we have a dynasty.

Gerbils tend to take over. Adjusting Thurber's remark, you find that you have gerbils like some people have gerbils. If you are an old gerbil-hand, forgive my novice enthusiasm. I am not, really, much of a Pet Lover. But how can these creatures, who must have been designed by a nursery toy-maker, so infuriatingly captivating are they, be resisted?

Of course they are rodents, like the nasty rat and the

dirty house mouse. How unjust we are in our judgements of animals. Merely because the gerbil is pretty as a picture postcard character, it wins one's heart and mind.

They were originally shipped in from Mongolia's deserts only fifteen years ago for laboratory research. Who conceivably could have infected or dissected a gerbil?

Fawn and white, with a shampooed look, they sit squirrel-fashion nibbling a sunflower seed held in hand like a corncob. Whiskers tweak with curiosity. Enormous eyes regard you, radiant as those of a girl being kissed for the first time.

They are bold, adventurous, confiding and brimming with affection. Admittedly they occasionally eat their babies—but, it seems to me, only when one has inadvertently disturbed their nest for a cleaning operation and without at first realizing that there has been another brood born. It is not, I believe, monstrous greed but an instinctive act of protection.

Usually the moment I enter the office they recognize my approaching footsteps and run up to the wire netting and rub noses on my finger tip. They amuse themselves by whizzing around in a little runged wheel, but their idea of unlimited fun is to have a cardboard tube from a paper towel roll dropped in. They slide up and down it like a tunnel of love, and emerge from the ends like corks from a pop-gun. While one is thus engaged, another couple will be starting on either end, crunching at it with their teeth like brandysnap and carrying off the shreds to add to their mountainous nests.

No, I have not been appointed PRO for Gerbils' Lib. Actually I do retain reservations about them. Not only do they reproduce at a bewildering rate (how has the world fought off a total take-over?), but they do stare so. And, frankly, as I noticed coming in from a distance and a change of atmosphere, they whiff a bit, too.

*

The prize was for 'the Competitor of any age who shall best dyke and plash one-and-a-half perch of hedge'. That's not a contest many of us could buckle down to, is it? Am I alone in, for a start, not even being able to measure a perch of anything, although I have turned my hand to a bit of amateur plashing before now.

In fact in the big sweep of South Wessex there are few left who can dyke and plash professionally. Why bother with such a laborious and fastidious craft when a mechanical cutter can munch a hedge down to the roots in a fraction of the time?

Only three of the old school turned up to tackle a scraggy and rattleboned overgrown stretch on Mr. Powell's land. It was a pleasure to squat on the lane bank in the pale golden glitter and watch them using hatchet and billhook with such precision and care.

Once probably a hundred different styles of bill were made locally throughout Britain. Ours has a longish and narrow blade. It is not an easy tool to use delicately, and at the speed at which these three went. Trimmed of branchlets, each stem of hazel or thorn in the hedge was slashed four-fifths through near the base. Then it was gently bent almost horizontal so that a hinge was left for the sap to rise through. At two-foot intervals chestnut stakes were driven in, and the stem was plashed (that is, pleached or woven) into a cowproof lattice.

The benign mood and sense of harmony which was mellow in my head as I sat and watched was, I concede, not entirely due to the occasion or to the tang of blackberries in the air. Other fruit had been at work upon my spirits. Earlier, in the tent next to a red-and-white stall selling Fair and Mop Rock and Sugar Boilings, as well as Cough Candy, Gingerbread, Liquorice Allsorts and Coconut Mushrooms, had been the home-made wine enclosure.

Such a selection! Did you know that good rosé wine can be made from rose petals, and a sort of hock from mint or maize or parsley or honeysuckle? It was the rose-petal rosé I bought and drank with my bread and cheese before the ploughing and plashing contests.

Ditch cleared and his section as neat as a row of barrackroom beds, Bill Miller from Punnel wiped the sweat from his forehead. 'I like blackthorn better. White-horn splits—it laughs at ee.' He pointed at the raw wood, splintered into a grinning mouth. Ash was awkward, too: you had to watch that it didn't snap off. But there was a tight hedge, for you.

On the adjoining huge tract the tractors were bustling up and down their allocated acreage, 'casting abroad and gathering together' the chocolate furrows. Gulls floated like smoke in their wake.

It was a battle. The ground had a cement crust and broke dustily after the dry spell, but the twenty-eight entries made a record for the Melplash Agricultural Society, going since 1847. Wessex used not to be noted for good ploughing. This was, above all, sheep country. The Dorset Horn was a hardy breed and, although it could live on poor pasture, it produced splendid mutton and its fleece of fine wool weighed four pounds.

At the peak of Wessex sheep-farming in the late 18th century there were 800,000 sheep grazing our downs—a figure which had slumped to 300,000 by 1900. Most of the enclosed land was sheep pasture: 50,000 acres of water-meadow and 290,000 of ewe leas and downs, with additional tillage where the ewes wintered. Sheep were all important, so other forms of agriculture stayed backward. One surveyor found the crude wooden ploughs drawn by six yoked oxen 'careless and insufficient'.

Down here there are still a farm or two using horses. But there is a new brilliant skill in the countryside now: prismatic metal in the fields. Big four-farrow Leylands and David Brown Selectamatics, McCormick Internationals and Fordson Supermajors breasted the Vale's skyline, red-and-white and all-scarlet, some with sky-blue cabins, others painted cream with Oxford blue piping. Their 'shears' (that's what the ploughshares are still called) flashed as they turned.

The Young Farmers' Club members were long-haired as King's Road boulevarders—or as medieval ploughboys.

Next door Bill Miller swung and plaited with a technique probably little altered since Anglo-Saxons began joining up natural fencing for their cattle. Engine throbbing, Dick Hurford on his steel saddle took four cups and certificates. His were adjudged to be the Best Strike-Out and Best Finish, with his Massey-Ferguson tractor and a Ransome hydraulic plough loaded with a heavy weight to thrust it into the armoured earth.

'If it'd been wetter I could have got some lovely furrows,' he said, 'but I don't reckon it came out too bad with the soil as it is. It shouldn't make too bad a seed bed.'

*

Half-heartedly I was plucking away rags and tatters of stems bunging up the guttering over the mill room, while a boisterous wind whirled them about the sky and, I suspected, then depositing them in a drainage ditch.

The house, I know, is untidy as a starling's nest. The stone and slate with which it was built, piecemeal, during the past four hundred years are covered like an old tramp wraps himself in layers of brown paper and odd garments.

Honeysuckle and wistaria and Virginia creeper and winter jasmine and clematis swarm and throttle each other. On one wall an old fig bulges pot-bellied over the pathway and blindfolds the windows of the barn loft which my young son converted into a studio, a shuddering chamber of rock music. A vine whose grapes never swell bigger than chick peas has shoved aside a drainpipe with its trunk.

Ivy insinuates under the coping and pallid stems grope

like blind fingers inside the stables. A flourishing bay beside the front door tops the chimney pot, and for all I know may be sealing it off. Everywhere there are ancient roses gone to briar, with stalks like the stiff, knotty, knobbly legs of Donald McGill dads paddling at Blackpool.

It is profligacy run riot, a fever of fructification; I know it to be a disgrace by good housekeeping standards. I am the sort of gardener who is held up to contempt and ridicule to tyro gardeners in books about gardening. I forget to prune at the right time, and when I do remember my secateurs pause at clumps so suited for a wren or robin or spotted flycatcher to build in.

Candidly, I like tufts of fern in crevices and moss on flagstones and lichens on the roof, those gaudy splashes of saffron and greeny-blue which are clusters of tiny rosettes.

You know what those lichens are busy doing? I try not to think about it. They are pioneers, commando squads of wreckers sent out ahead. They secrete an acid which slowly dissolves rock and slate. Pockets of humus accumulate. They are little pouches of moisture and they feed on the roots of high plants, so they are for ever expanding the frontiers of life, preparing the ground for bigger growth. I am being gnawed away at from all directions.

And yet, you see, I think a house should be lived on as well as in. It should be an organic part of its surroundings.

In one of his books Desmond Morris has much to say about the importance of touch in the relationship between people (and he was taken to task in some quarters for imprecisely confusing intimacy with proximity). What I thought was missing from his considerations was the tactile satisfaction in the contact between human flesh and non-human things, fingers in soil, on wood, against rock.

Personally I get no sensuous pleasure from the feel of plastic or nylon or fibreglass or cement, although I know

I am in a diminishing minority and that such materials are opening new scope for the artist and sculptor.

No, I prefer the grain of bark, the polish put on floor tiles by boot studs, the patina of old brick, the texture of stone seamed and sandpapered by weather.

'Happiness is a warm gun' was the Western outlaw's aesthetic. I wouldn't go quite to the opposite extreme of saying 'Happiness is a damp, decayed autumn leaf', I thought as I clawed out sopping handfuls from the guttering, swaying on my ladder in the blustery October wind, but that is nearer the truth for me.

November

I NIPPED out for wood, to kindle the ash still glowing from yesterday's fire on the stone flags of the sitting room ingle (it burns without smoking, so the bay tree can't yet have quite smothered the chimney top) . . . Getting ready for a bit of telly-viewing. Such excitement in store.

BBC2 cannot penetrate our valley fastness. Colour has never been glimpsed. BBC1 comes in blurrily through a blizzard of static. On our regional commercial station we see, scratchily, ads for car marts far down the coast and scenes shot in smart candle-lit restaurants frequented by the *beau monde* of Plymouth.

French programmes jabber dominantly on our screen, and there are occult images which are said to float in from Madrid. I am thinking of demanding my licence fee back from the government and declaring a TV UDI.

Still, I obstinately switch on the set if there is something which promises to be worth viewing. If all I can see are cosmic explosions, then I can chuck it in. If the interference is aggressive and the signal feeble, I shall, instead, read in front of the crackling apple branches which smell like warm cider as they burn, and start burrowing into the piles of books put to one side for such occasional evenings away from the desk.

Viewing or reading, whichever—first a big blaze, so out to the skillen, the open-sided wood store behind the kitchen. The cords of logs sawn on hot June days have already shrunk, gulped by that cavernous fireplace. I picked a chunky piece remaining from one depleted stack—and saw that I had taken the roof off some lodgers.

Two wood mice scuttled out. They didn't go far. They ran along a bridge of lichen-tufted twigs, turned and chirruped at me indignantly.

They were very fetching. They had silky auburn coats and white shirt fronts, elegantly long tails, and absurd ears sticking up like pink arum lilies. Their noses, tapering like Concorde's, vibrated with fine sprightly whiskers. They regarded me anxiously with enormous bright eyes.

I saw why they were so fretted. I had lifted the lid off their pantry. In a nook among the litter was a deposit account of food, their modest Fort Knox of assets for the lean months: larch seeds, beechmast and kibbled maize pinched, without a doubt, from the sack in the dovecote.

We eyed each other for a couple of seconds. After vacillating, and after they had flipped out of sight, I replaced the log I was holding and took in an armful from another pile, scoffing at my sentimentality. No argument, I was falling for a pretty face. I would not have been so indulgent had they been rats or wood lice.

To be realistic, I knew that the wood mouse (oftener in hedgerows and field edges than in woods) may not be guilty of breaking and entering your premises, but it will chew up the peas in your vegetable plot with jaws whirring like a waste disposal unit. It digs down and deguts crocus bulbs. If you have noticed the frayed hems of sprouting wheat fields you will understand why farmers do not treasure the wood mice which live in the adjoining rouets of the headlands where the plough turns, and in the rough grass of the gawls too hummocky for sowing.

Furthermore, although an outdoor type and for ever fussily washing, it is a spectacularly lousy mouse. It has been found to be host to nine species of flea, plus assorted lice and mites, and ten different intestinal worms.

Still, my feelings were tinged with autumnal solicitude. Earlier a few laggardly house martins had been hunting through the yellow leaves drifting down into the river—perhaps their very last meal in English skies before flying out to sea and Africa, surely the last of the swallow family I shall see this year.

The countryside is suddenly drained and emptier. There is, I think, room for the wood mice under my roof.

*

Descending from the village on the hill was like merging into a landscape painting still wet and runny: the dribbling away, the bleeding off, of colours as the remaining leaves twirled down from the roadside ashes and sycamores. Those high on the foothills, the flight of wide grassy steps climbing to Haggerdown, were already stripped nearly bare by the unobstructed winds up there.

I was born in Yorkshire and my thinning blood still quickens to the bare muscularity of the Pennines, to Auden's definition of 'a faultless love':

. . . what I hear is the murmur
Of underground streams, what I see is a limestone landscape.

And when I lived in East Anglia I got pleasure, of a different sort but as keen, from the enormous skies and fenny flatness.

But I am happiest here in the intricate and moody countryside of South Wessex. There is nowhere like it, this one hundred square miles bounded on one side by the Great Heath—Hardy's 'haggard waste of Egdon'—and on the other by the Great Marsh.

Crushed between are terminating rock seams from east and north, colliding in a mad pile-up. There is a tumbled anarchy of hills, contracted Pyrenees: long hogbacks of chalk, sheer limestone scarps, billows of down, knaps and knolls and batches, and high conelets of sandstone like emerald plum puddings.

Some visitors are uneasy. It is not just a matter of being swallowed in the remoteness and haunted antiquity of the land. There is also the sense of being conjured with, of hallucination. It is halls of mirrors in series and in receding rows, with results like the reversal of the expected in a Magritte painting. Take two steps in any direction and your surroundings are rearranged like the painted scenery of a toy theatre.

It is a geological madhouse. A new hummock inflates before your eyes; an unsuspected valley has unfolded. It is easy to feel disorientated. It is also, if you enjoy it, easy to allow yourself to be lost.

Old green-roads and droveways and tangled tracks wind into mysterious furzy coombs where on a summer afternoon you hear nothing but the bees and the wail of a soaring buzzard, and in winter perhaps the bubbling trill of curlews flighting down to the estuary saltings.

Even in the touristy summer months the lanes aren't much used. Motorists eye them and turn tail, foreseeing a respray job after squeezing through those brambly clefts. So grass sprouts through the tarmacadam and some are dim tunnels roofed over by knitted boughs and draped with ferns.

But it is now that the hedgerows take a bad beating. Going back to the mill after a pub lunch at the Horseshoes, my passage was blocked by Tom. Tom keeps busy at almost anything, a bit of building, timber felling, boat repairs. Now he was hedging.

He was aboard a tractor which brandished the huge saw-tooth mandibles of a sci-fi ant. Its power blades were scrunching through the trunks, leaving an edge as low and squared-off as a high street kerb.

Tom is one of the few left hereabouts who can lay a hedge by hand in a comely manner—he can do that plashing, all right. He attended to my boundary quickset which had gone spindly. Now that the slashed and staked thorn branches, bent to forty-five degrees, have put out their vertical rails it is stockproof—and Suzy-proof—and stout as corrugated iron.

The difference is that the hedger with his billhook has an eye for detail. He lets through the wild-sown oak, so there is body left for the honeysuckle and briar, so food for insects and for birds. The mechanical cutter is not selective. Zzzzzzzzrrrrrr—and all is uniform, and emptier.

Understandably a good farmer wants the overhang trimmed back from his corn, but I regret seeing this secret country cropped bald. Understandably why should Tom or the farmer prefer the wet and wearisome—and much more costly in man-hours—method when it can be done in comfort and a fraction of the time?

Zzzzzzzzrrrrrr went the cutter, and the exhaust fumed in my face, as progress proceeded and the rest of the hedge bit the dust.

*

There is much more light everywhere. The November gales are now rioting down the valley on a hooligan binge, smashing open the frontage of the wood, ripping off the last decorations of leaves.

The field oaks still cling hard to their ragged orange shawls, and my beech hedge is still thick, a frozen bonfire of yellow and crimson flames. Most of its lower leaves, despite the winds to come, will stay on until pushed off by the spring's expanding buds. Those which fall make good compost because they are rich in potash—and we don't nowadays need them for mattress filling, excellently bouyant though they used to be found.

But the hanging wood on the slitheringly precipitous river bank is already stripped bare of smothering summer; even the sky has a scoured brightness, as if cleared of cloud by a metal rake. The row of poplars on the far hill are bristly as broomsticks.

I do not use that image thoughtlessly: not about those portals to witch country.

It is an odd area beyond the ridge, where the Great Marsh starts. It has never been settled in human history. In the far blue haze is the jagged tip of the Pen and its rock parapet. In front is a wide desolation crossed by nothing more solid than a cart track.

The scattered hydes and smallholdings have a run-down and withdrawn look. The few villages are isolated and drab. The floor of the plain is impermeable blue clay. Springs—those winter bournes—cannot effervesce through it. After autumn the rain lies and the land becomes a gummy slime. In this remoteness superstition tarries just as stagnantly.

To be found roundabout, and outside the perimeter of the vale, is the more conventional monkey business: a poltergeist record for the village next to mine, the case of a phantom murdered schoolboy in Emminster, and the famous 'screaming skull' at the large house near by. What interests me more is the place in everyday life of a reliance upon systems not formally accepted as workable.

My doctor, when called out into these parts, sometimes finds that a local 'charmer' has already been called in. Charmers are white witches. Much as it may need them, the National Health doesn't count them in. Nor do they belong to the Royal Veterinary College, but they are much employed when a cow has thunk (udder obstruction) or calves get husk, which is an infestation of the windpipe from eating too much wet grass.

Not all charmers benignly banish thunk and husk. There is a blacker variety of wizardry around here. In the vale heather grows in scarlet streaks on the rim of greensand, and the only sizeable village—sensibly pulling its skirts out of the mire up on to the hill slope—has a glorious church with Norman arches and early English carving. But the evil eye which may still be cast within sight of this tower probably comes from an even older vein of belief and knowledge.

I know of a family whose livestock sickened, whose crops died, whose health failed from worry. Why? Because, they were convinced, they had been 'auver-looked', that is overlooked or bewitched by a 'wise woman' or a 'cunning man', and it isn't long since that most villages had one or the other in residence, and perhaps a few still have. A vicar along the coast wrote in a book a year or two back about overlooking: 'This is equivalent to what in more primitive countries would be termed "the evil eye", but I honestly believe that where it does occur in this most beautiful part of Southern England it is more diabolical and all embracing . . . It is the power of staring on crops or animals with such intensity of devilish hatred that evil is said to descend on whatever the baleful gaze is directed at.' He described how his Christian blessings deflected curses being radiated upon a farm by an overlooker with 'cruel cadaverous face and wild unblinking eyes'.

As a matter of fact, it is not only animals and property which can be overlooked. There are many cases on record around here of individuals who languished and ailed because—they thought—of being overlooked, and who, acting in the spirit of Talbot in Shakespeare's *Henry VI*, where he threatens Joan la Pucelle: 'Blood will I draw on thee; thou art a witch', have attempted to draw blood on suspected neighbours with needles and even a billhook.

You may think that you have to put up with 'cruel cadaverous faces and wild unblinking eyes' every night from TV, but it is not a subject to be joked about—nor does it retreat from such new-fangled gadgets. The divine of whom I spoke is acquainted with a vet who arrived at a house as a cow was being led out of the front door. The local charmer was ill, so he had been rung up and the receiver held to the cow's ear while the incantation was recited.

The cow got better. That was not a recorded message. These lines of transmission recede beyond the GPO into a timeless era of communications. You must, however, be careful about what you mentally dial.

*

Nobody shakes my hand when making a repeat visit to the mill. That is not because they lack a genial welcome —well, not usually, although I confess that there have been occasions when, spotting an unfamiliar figure marching purposefully down the drive clutching what looks like the invitation to open a bazaar, I have taken to the tall timber and melted away into my environment.

But even a friend usually avoids that spontaneous hand-clasp, probably remembering that, a previous time, his palm sank into a lump of rancid suet or, with a whinny of nausea, he found his fingers laced with old bacon rind.

This is because, like an ungroomed waiter working out his notice in a restaurant struck off by Quentin Crewe, I am frequently bearing what some regard as goodies to a platter on the front lawn.

Greasy paw apart, it is probable that mouldy breadcrumbs have lodged like confetti in that shapeless Icelandic fisherman's sweater which clads me in winter, and that peanuts are dribbling from a trouser pocket. Not a pretty sight.

The bird table is nailed on top of a birch stump. It has the powerful reek of a gibbet. Soddened crusts have caked like putty in the crevices. A blackened hank of gristle, leathery as biltong, swings in the biting wind, as malefactors once did at the roadside.

How did the idea get abroad that bird tables are rather twee? Mine is more like an abattoir than a Wendy house. At the time of a strike by the dustmen I felt arguably to be within the dirty job pay category.

Why do I, in all weathers, trudge out with congealed scraps snatched from other people's plates? Because of the pleasure I get from the carnival activity around and upon it.

This morning, at one moment, eight varieties of bird were at the feast: three tits (blue, great and coal) doing their circus trapeze act on the nut hopper, a sleek nuthatch, a couple of starlings butchering pork left-overs, a blackbird and an aggressive robin trying to take over the whole programme.

They were scattered by a brilliant star shell, a hefty bird which shot in and clamped to the birch trunk with an audible thud. It was a great spotted woodpecker, parrot-bright in black, crimson and white togs. With its jemmy of a bill it rifled the nut basket like a safecracker.

I make extravagant claims for what I classify as my garden birds. As the mill is surrounded by farm meadows and wild hillsides, birds therefore discern no frontiers: it is all one to them. So this year alone I have spotted forty-eight different species around the house—including a particularly rare one, a tawny pipit, on migration, and the dippers whose young fluttered into the hall from their moss igloo beside my weir. There can't, I'm sure, be many people with dippers as house guests.

Those magpies built in the old juniper outside my writing room, and kestrels bred in a broken elm over the hedge. I even appropriate the buzzard, for seldom does a day go by without one or more of the three pairs in this valley gliding overhead on galleon sail wings.

I have no wish to tame my callers—the feathered ones, I mean. I am privileged to have sight of them going about their private business. But I do try to attract them by lending a hand with extra rations now that frosts begin to snap and natural food supplies thin.

There is a hard streak of self-interest in this Lady Bountiful behaviour, I do admit. Those scroungers which come for the mixed finch seed or coconut will stay in spring, perhaps. Then they forage for themselves.

And one pair of, say, wrens will stuff down their chicks' gullets more than one thousand insects daily—

caterpillars and fly larvae which a gardener wants to see the back of.

A pair of wrens is a far better investment than a can of poison spray.

*

There are moments (they pass) when I think wistfully of the peace and quiet of town: the placid orderliness of inhabiting a high-rise flat, plugged into all the mechanical solutions for everyday problems.

Living in the country is so fraught. Nature springs surprises like the prizefighter's jab you didn't see coming. Anxieties bloom like antirrhinums; despair under the elms; neuroses round the door.

You will recall my agitation about a population explosion of a floating plant casually introduced to the lower leat. That voluptuous green eiderdown spread madly across the surface and my fear was for the rainbow trout, that they would have suffocated, sealed up in those airless deeps. They survived. But I have to make regular sweeps, trawling it with an old sheet, scooping off the persistent stuff.

I pamper the trout. I feed them on stinky pellets which seem to be caviar to them—if that's not a cruelly thoughtless remark to make about a fish. As I leaned on the footbridge iron rail, flicking in their snacks, they came rushing through the water lily stems, leaping and grabbing like nautical leopards.

That is how it used to be. Now fewer come. And that is not just because they are sluggish with autumn. My gladness that the trout recovered from the take-over bid of that American water fern is shared by another. There is a daily visit from this gaunt, grey fish-lover who stands on the bank peering fondly down at his favourites, that heron I had already had suspicions about.

How many of my speckled beauties have gone into that scrawny craw? It puts a strain upon my alleged love for birds to embrace this uninvited visitor, bearing its long dagger of horn, elegant though it is in a leggy, lean, *Vogue* model way.

On the bedroom window seat now is my shot gun. No, I have no intention of pumping the heron full of lead. I merely want to put a warning blast across its murderous prow. The rude shock may encourage it to poach elsewhere.

But I can never spot it! Along the bank are only clotted hanks of dead stems of meadowsweet and rushes and reedmace. Yet into this meagre cover the heron merges invisibly like a jungle guerilla.

When I awake I seize the gun and peer stealthily through the open window. I look out into a pearly Eden, a filigree of boughs and stalks sequinned with glinting dew, a marquetry of webs and fine yashmaks of mist. It is all silent and hooded. The frogging of rushes is silvery with frost; the water is black as satin. But it is blank—apparently—of a heron. I decide, once again, that I am too late or that the heron on this morning has given me a miss.

Then, as I draw back the curtains, this thirty-six inches of bird manifests itself only fifteen yards away, a ghost taken form from shadow and ripple, and off it fans on vast wings which it has conjured out of its folded umbrella body.

It is delightful that some herons have set up a community in London, on the Regent's Park lake island, safe from interference. It must be so harmonious and peaceful for all concerned, up there in the middle of the metropolis. I wish this rustic heron could see the good sense of that.

*

My Dataday diary, full of worthy printed entries for socially-conscious citizens such as 'Election Day USA' and 'United Nations Day', passed by Martinmas without so much as a mention.

It shall not go entirely unnoticed and unhonoured. How deplorable that so handyman a saint, of a variety of service to all sorts, should be given the go-by. Martin was a humanitarian as 4th-century ecclesiastics went. Although anti-heathen, he refused to be associated with the bishops who sanctioned the execution of heretics at Trèves in 385.

All that may seem far in years and geography from my hole-up in the West Country in the 1970s. Not really. Martin, when a rough soldier and still a catechumen, had a vision of Christ after, on a chill night, ripping his cloak to give half of it to a beggar.

After that, I'll have you know, the sun beamed again to mark his deed of charity. So Martin remains the saint of tramps as well as of husbandmen. For, at harvest's end, a sunny November 11 can herald St. Martin's Little Summer, the mild and mellow interlude following the first cold assault.

So it has been here. Golden days. Without a breeze stirring, the final few leaves fluttered down from the lime on the lawn, great titian snowflakes. Drifts are everywhere: the copper shreds of beech, yellow slivers from the poplars, singed moths from the birches on the common.

Pheasants, bronze and scarlet as autumn itself, peregrinate far from the woods to feed on the stubble. Across the calm blue hurl volleys of iron arrowheads, starlings. There are still a few weakling blooms of loosestrife, but the brilliance now shines from the rose-hips and the berries of the alder buckthorn by the brook.

I have heard the voices of hounds on the wind. The hunt killed eighty brace of foxes in the last September to April season; nearly two hundred others were shot in the locality, including the ninety knocked off by Bob, the gamekeeper.

Amazingly, foxes are still common. They saunter through my paddock (where they are neither shot nor hunted, except occasionally by those frisky heifers), tiptoeing fussily, but without bothering about concealment, through the dewy grass.

Last night the vocal battle of some tawny owls in the beech wood was joined by a vixen's shrill howl. Already mating begins again.

So the earth renews itself as it subsides, and the gap is bridged by the tranquil warmth of the heteroclite summer which St. Martin keeps in store.

He was, incidentally, a jolly chap as well as pious. The Church allocated as the day to be dedicated to him an old pagan festival where there was much boozing, possibly in the hope of obliterating the older custom. Instead, as is so often the case, it was merely absorbed. So St. Martin is also the patron of carousing gatherings and of reformed drunkards.

Reformed? Well, it is quite in order to toast Martin with the cider made from our potent apples.

*

Ceiling zero, ground porridge-o. Rain thudding like fists on the window panes. Clouds ebony as crows belting across the Knoll.

The gale hurtles, in real blow-blow-thou-winter-wind-freeze-freeze-thou-bitter-sky style, down the valley. It booms through the wood. It tears off the worn-out undergarments of foliage, leaving the trees at last naked and shivering. This is no strip-tease; this is assault and battery.

I had barely finished writing about the benign sunny lull when the rough weather barged in. I don't mind. I enjoy the drama, the stormy space turbulent with black boughs and careering leaves—watching it all from the window, that is.

Also I enjoy the feel of the land's endurance when, with summer's fat pared off, it braces bone and sinew against the pummelling. One glimpses this wild country as Hardy's Jude Fawley saw it when the 'sad wet seasons' lowered upon his hard 'upland world'.

It is the time, too, to watch for wanderers buffeted off track from their passage along the coast.

I buttoned the parka up to the neck and went out. It seemed effete, cuddling up to the central heating when I could see my neighbour herding his cattle across the far rim of hills. I could make a gesture and tidy up the strewn twigs from the lawn.

It was not a joyful scene. The last sweet sediment of the year's fruitfulness had drained and gone, and it was a grey hollowness which was left. In the soggy chiaroscuro silence there seemed to be only one thing alive: a rather nasty fungus sprouting under the lime. Without noticing it, as I dragged together the debris of broken branches, my hand touched it, and was snatched away: it had the corpse touch of a toad.

As I regarded its unpleasantly creamy cone an unfamiliar chirping brought up my eyes. A rook was chasing a small delta-wing shape, or trying to. The other was much too fast. The rook gave up and tottered back to its tribe feeding on the sheeplease. The pursued, still chattering irritably, shot overhead, a compact bird with the flash of a cutlass blade.

Clearly it was a hawk. Automatically my mind whizzed through the elimination process. Too small for a kestrel; too sharp-winged and short-tailed for a sparrow-hawk; the hobbys which bred near by have long since migrated.

It had an odd flicking flight, showing first pale chest and then dark back.

Identification narrowed down to a falcon which nests no nearer than Dartmoor, and there only sparsely, and which I have seen but twice previously: a merlin.

Dropping the twigs, I sped to my bookshelves for consultation with the masters. I am only too well aware of the multitude of confusions which can lead one astray and yet I still think it was a merlin which passed over my garden. I had it in view for five seconds in murky light. It is impossible to be sure. And one always must sternly counteract the subconscious hope that it is an exciting rarity which has cropped up.

Bird-sightings are often as tantalizingly momentary. I always seem to have left my field-glasses behind at the most vital moments. But I am glad that I decided not to frowst indoors—you can never tell what the wind may bring your way.

*

I didn't dare mention it until summer was over. Now the evidence is destroyed, part of the putrefaction which overtook all the year's frills and conceits of lacy leaves and the flowers' scented purses. Gone to dust, every one —including my guilty secret.

Back in sultry August I was pacing the garden with a colleague. Although a television producer, he is a trained botanist. You see what happens to our science graduates.

We stopped on the footbridge. The mill stream was moving like molasses through the ravine. Golden-green horse flies were using the water lily pads as pontoons, too flaked out in the sluggish heat to take to wing.

Our script discussion became desultory. Leaning on the rail, I gazed, rather glazedly, at the depths to see if the trout were bestirring themselves, or if there was any sign of the solitary pale carp which sometimes goes through the underwater woods of weed. I watched the red admirals feeding on the purple flowers frothing in tall clumps on the bank and leaning almost into the water.

'What sort of valerian is that?' I asked. It seemed to me to be quite like the spur valerian which grows from crevices in the stone walls of the barns, and whose seeds are said to have arrived in the boot welts of Roman legionnaires. (I doubt that.)

'That's no valerian,' said my knowledgeable friend. 'That's a fine crop of hemp you've got—*eupatorium cannabinum.*'

I looked back to the plant. I sniffed the air. Good grief, was I wide open for a cannabis rap? He explained. This was hemp agrimony, the remotest relative of the pot producer, but not without its own potency, I gathered. The name agrimony derives from Greek for cataract, and it makes a powerfully good ointment which is probably among the medicines of those surreptitious apothecaries, the white witches, of the Vale country. A tuft of this has for long been regarded as, you might say, a site for sore eyes.

I was reminded of the medicaments which sprout from our soil by a correspondent's letter describing how a gipsy had cured an eczema which had defeated specialists. Her prescription was to crush the leaves of 'rosettes'—house leeks—and mix with cream. And, she declared, it had worked.

It so happened that since my trip to the Pacific in the winter I had had a scaly area on my hand which foiled National Health unguents. I have house leeks on the premises, the *sempervivum tectorum*, which spreads its fleshy wreaths on the roof tiles and in crevices in the garden walls. In the fridge was cream. What had I to lose? Only my festering patch. Accordingly I went to grinding and mixing, and daubed on the resulting green slush.

A week later my skin was fair as it ever was. I do not ask you to gasp with astonishment. I merely report the facts.

I have jotted this in the flyleaf of my booklet of 17th-century Wessex herbal remedies. One goes: 'Take a nuttmegg and a little large mace pound this small and mix them with a little treakle put them in a linnin bagg warm it and lay it to the temples.'

This is 'To caus sleep'. You can say that again. Nowadays it would be called getting high. For, like morning glory seeds and some mushrooms, nutmeg has been a vehicle for tripping on since time immemorial—like hemp.

Our ancestors, I fear, knew not only their leeks and

onions. They were also familiar with sources of dreams and visions which are now manufactured in black market laboratories.

*

And while I am about it, there is another thing which has been on my mind and which really ought to be cleared up—those rather beastly words I wrote earlier about the four foul-mouthed leftovers hanging about the mill, the guineafowl which glowered from the walls, razzed the dogs from out-of-reach branches, and skulked at the laneside like footpads.

Despite the guineafowls' ridiculous appearance—like a Blackpool postcard fat lady, wide-hipped and with a little, petulant, rouge-dabbed face—and their uncouth rowdiness and nagging tongues which shattered sunny evenings, I have been shamed into eating my cruel words.

How can I convey the pathos of what followed? On a chill sleeting afternoon I was reading in my warm study. Outside on the balcony I heard a strange dulcet trill, low and tender. Puzzled, I stepped to the French door and peeped through the window pane.

Huddled together were two of the guineafowl. They looked slatternly and unhappy. And they were murmuring consolingly to each other in a mellifluous undertone.

Obviously their chums had been bumped off. Someone had had a toughish roast. Or perhaps a sly fox had at last managed to jump them. Now the survivors had come home again and were singing like obese canaries. I was quite touched. With the easy living of high summer gone, they had returned to the old homestead for succour.

There were some stale biscuits in a tin in the study. I sprinkled them on the tiles outside. That's how I was unScrooged. Now a touch brusquely, I feed them daily from a corn bag kept on the *Encyclopaedia Britannica*. Sometimes I am strongly tempted to throw the LIBI to MARY volume at them, but it is too late.

They have accepted me. They and my dogs have accepted each other. Every day there used to be that repeat show of the same melodrama. The quartet flew to roost in the lime and hurled vituperation at the dogs. The dogs galloped like raiding Redskins around the tree, whooping insanely. No one got anywhere.

Gradually the heat went out. The dogs' attack lost its passion; the note of outrage in the guineafowls' squawks became less convincing. The beagle began slouching down the path without a sideward glance, the birds no more than paused momentarily from pecking around on the lawn.

The factor which had entered was that which has saved many tribes and nations from exterminating one another: boredom. Does this story have a happy ending, of harmony and love in a mixed society?

Not quite. Those beady eyes fixed on me from the balcony rail are expressing not devotion but hope of another hand-out. Still, there is a tacit agreement to live side by side without quarrel, and that is a situation which is not to be undervalued. And they do sing prettily to each other.

December

I TOOK a tentative look through the rain-smeared window at the valley in the light of dawn. (Already I had been three hours at the desk.)

It looked as inviting as an execution shed: a sky daubed grey with government-issue distemper, trees as gaunt as girders.

I do not mention being up this early in a bragging spirit. I had set the alarm clock peevishly, driven to the desperate move only by the deadline for an article which hung around my neck like a rope. The outlook could not have been more appropriate. The condemned man prepared to eat a hearty breakfast.

Just before I repaired downstairs to the frying pan, I was cheered to see that someone else was as unhappy as I. A distressed screech and the hoarse clamour of a mob drew my eye to a skirmish above the brushy gorge where the river runs. That heron, flapping in for some more of my trout, had been spotted by the rooks, now back at their beech wood colony after wandering away in the late summer.

The next couple of minutes supplied the excitement of a Battle of Britain film sequence. Lumbering along on its vast wings, the heron heeled sideways like a heavy bomber evading fighters. The rooks circled up into attack formation, then peeled off in turn to swoop—black Hurricanes—on to the enemy. Their vindictive throaty cries had the clatter of Vickers guns as they dived.

Each strike (or pretended strike) sent the heron flailing down. Then it staggered back up the sky, stilt legs askew and long neck hunched into shoulders like a pilot hoping glumly to butt his way out of the battle.

As far as I could see, neither heron nor rook lost a single feather. It was all a ferocious charade.

The heron is no innocent. Almost anything moving will be speared by that massive blade of a bill—trout or toad, rat or grasshopper, moorhen or grass snake. I still don't care for the attention this one pays to my mill pond although I'm pretty sure that the rainbow trout which stayed alive are now big enough to fend for themselves, but the few small carp I put in earlier haven't been seen for months and I know why.

The rooks, with their system of collective security in their tree-top township, have least cause of all to get trigger-happy. So why do they fume so? Why do they give that heron—which on most days is delving somewhere along the valley's trellis of streams—such a bad time?

Perhaps it looks menacingly hawk-like on that big wing-spread. And yet I don't think that is the explanation. The heron is grey in spirit as well as in colouring, a melancholy character; it is a surly old tramp, and so it is picked upon by a crowd of rowdies, and pelted and jeered out of the street.

I watched it plugging away along the hill frontage. The rooks returned jauntily to their perches with much self-satisfied croaking.

Had they thought themselves endangered? Not a bit. They were deliberately making a ridiculous fuss at the invasion of their territorial air space, and enjoying every second of their litigious indignation and outraged rights.

That is not an entirely strange mode of behaviour—nor is it confined to ornithological circles.

*

'Come and see the priest hole,' I said to a London guest.

I led him across the granite flags, worn concave by the boots of generations of millers and their lads, to the far end of the hall, and raised the trap door.

'I didn't know that they had frogmen priests—I suppose what nowadays we call water-canon,' my sophisticated friend said wittily. He is so full of townish neuroses that I suspect he would not sit in a laundromat for fear of catching pneumonia.

Nevertheless I pushed him aside and, in an access of fright, peered apprehensively over his shoulder into the square of darkness. I was not equally amused to see greenish bilge lapping thigh-deep at the stone walls of that cosy chamber originally built for a papist drop-out. It now looked like the Paris sewers in *Les Miserables*.

Hastily I dropped the lid, closing it upon reality. I knew what had happened. After damming the disused millpond at the back of the house to raise the water to its old mark, it had seeped through the masonry into this little cavity below ground level.

This is but one detail in the intricate hydraulic system embrangled around this building, over which many a plumbing engineer has brooded then walked away despondently, gnawn by self-doubt and wondering where his career went wrong.

Our water supply derives from a spring in the hillside, in a dingle where in April primroses cluster in an Arthur Rackham bower of meshed branches, mossy logs and cool fern fronds, a place which is dreamy and a touch sinister: it is that cloying smell of decay of countless rotted layers of life, which the bubble of the stream and the gay songs of willow tits and warblers do not disperse even on days of sunbeams and flowers.

The water surfaces again in my garden, in an entanglement of lead pipes which are coiled like a basket of snakes against the north wall. If you pull one particular pipe toward you, out spouts water. I am told that while it dribbles, all is well: the walls will stand, the kingdom will prevail.

I am content to leave it at that. I do not interfere with anything in the mill room. The big wooden wheel crumbled to dust long ago. In the Thirties an occupant decided to tap the latent power from the upper leat's fifteen-foot head of water stacked inside the culvert.

He installed a turbine generator. It looms there still in the half-light, a monstrous black riddle of pipes and cogs and sluice valves, a museum piece from an earlier machine age. Once I experimentally gave a few turns to a rusted handwheel. A rumble in the iron guts. A great breathy growl. Things began to clank into motion.

Would it burst its rivets, tear itself from its moorings and clump down the valley, the Rogue Dynamo That Stalks By Night? Terrified, I jerked back the wheel to where it had been. The grunting and grinding subsided with a wheeze . . . a gasp of regret or a muttered threat?

I retreated from it and crossed the grating, through which you can see the heave of water under your feet, pushing onward through that brick colon to the bright world beyond.

On a shelf above the panel of dials I found a pile of documents. In yellowed envelopes were bundles of papers, and among them a Kingsway firm's tender, bound in maroon covers, which itemized such parts as 'One stuffing box cast iron with split gland.' Had I been meddling with the stuffing box? Had I touched a nerve in the sensitive split gland?

There also was a packet of nineteen—yes, nineteen—blueprints from which, you might think, could be constructed an ABM Sentinel System for the nation. In fact, I have been told by those who remember that when the plant was really making things hum at full pitch of youthful vigour, it supplied one-and-a-half hours of brownish orange wavering light per evening.

Later they stuck pylons across the country, perceptively picking the most open and prominent places so that everyone could share the aesthetic drama of the handsome Meccano skyscrapers. So mains electricity came to these valleys, and the millrace had no purpose—except to be beautiful and spread embracingly and fondly into my cellars.

A trifle unnerved at what had been revealed by my conducted tour of the priest hole, I left my friend with a drink in the drawing room and I went outside to my oracular pipe. I drew it down from the wall. Unhesitatingly it gushed. I think we may bail ourselves out.

*

They really do make one feel a ragabash, just a scruffy jack-by-the-hedge, as they pass in casual procession at a stately clop-clop-clop.

Such *sang-froid*, such splendour! Coats of dark blue, or black, or the red called pink, with white stocks; breeches of cream or fawn; boots conker-bright. Flat almost brimless bowlers. Brown or black velvet hats, some with chin-straps. Quite a few toppers.

All the pony-mounted young girls in worn tweed hacking jackets are pretty. The ladies, hair girded in nets, are without exception beautiful. The men on towering chestnut thoroughbreds are boldly handsome.

The hounds, tongues hanging, tails swaying, surge up the lane to the gathering beside the church. The gargoyles grin down upon the prologue, between the thatched cottages and the sere bramble leaves, of the passion play to come.

Greetings are exchanged. Laughter. Snorting of horses, chink and creak of metal and leather. A dewy morning. The wan sun strikes blinding stars from spiders' webs and brass buttons.

Master in front, they set off: a stylish, swashbuckling army with animals eager and strong of leg, seventy mettlesome country people, streaming like a brilliant banner into the dun root field, stirrup cup inside them, sharp December wind on their faces.

Through a gateway (quickly a morass, mud spuming up from hooves) 'to a cowy pasture yonder', a villager who has been stopping earths tells me, to get a quarry up on his pads for the great chase.

It crosses my mind that the fine army is somewhat loaded against the object of the exercise: a rufous, poodle-sized wild dog which, it is hoped, after being bolted up from its daytime snooze and racing on a blazing scent, will be bitten to death. This hunt 'accounts for' eighty brace of foxes in the season, by being out three days a week.

I am not a haunter of hunts; I do not ride to hounds. The meet is near by on the county's northern boundary, in the clay valleys broken by steep ripples of cornbrash. So I crossed the chalk ridge to have a look.

From a tor, where the country is getting moorlandish with brake-fern and heather, I have a grandstand place above the arable and spinneys. The whipper-in, a scarlet exclamation mark where a sentence of hedgerow ends, stands sentry while the huntsman draws a covert.

The grumbling of disturbed rooks is drowned by the pack giving tongue. Barbaric yawp of horn. There is a find. View hulloa! Riders pound in silhouette across the low hooping hill. The sixteen-and-a-half couples of bitches are crying on a line. The roused fox—a 'straight-necked' one—streaks across the grass and dodges among young spruce.

The hounds persevere; they are tidily bunched and running well, but their tails are pale pennants over the scrub as they mill about with the scent failed. The fox is away again. Horses thunder, flicking sweat and front down the lanes, to head him. But he is across the railway line and in deeper undergrowth.

I am more worn out than the hounds. Ninety minutes gone. We are at the far end of the Forestry Commission plantations, where the land slopes into Somerset.

A sign—this is Coker Wood!

Back home, fox given best, hunt left pursuing further

arduous pleasure, I thumb through to the lines which came to my mind, those in T. S. Eliot's *Four Quartets* which follow 'East Coker':

We shall not cease from exploration
And the end of all our exploring
Will be to arrive where we started
And know the place for the first time.

*

A kestrel breasted the freezing sea wind and hung, wings hooked, in the glinting space of sun and sky, a dark anchor. Huddled deep into my fleece collar under the lee of Haggerdown, I felt to be able to see as the hunting falcon saw, but through the intense present into the past.

All of Wessex seemed to stretch away below, swelling and flattening through valleys and low hills to the Chase, to the smoky blueness of the Wiltshire chalk uplands. It could not have looked much different to the successive waves of skin-clothed nomads, Roman infantry-men, and Saxon and Jute settlers.

Where there was unbroken forest there are hedges, now shining with the swansdown of traveller's joy. Heathland has been cultivated, marshes drained, timber plantations set over bogs, downland hacked back; but the contours of wind-gaps and dips notching the sweeping bare heights are the same.

The solitude and loveliness cannot be much less today than at any time when the eye and heart of Englishmen quickened to this homeland.

I could see my own village, slate roofs, grey stone spire; other hamlets and farmsteads and linnedges were scattered in between. I could see the deep pleats of old oak forest, washed around by a henna surf of dead bracken and mounting to rough dune-like wasteland where last spring a pair of rare hawks, Montagu's harriers, nested. They had hunted the earthworks immediately below me, the home of the spider orchid and the harebell. I know nowhere else left in all of Britain where the butterflies stripe the lanes with such rich colour in the still summer heat.

This is where the American oil corporation is being allowed to go ahead and drill—for the protestors' funeral for the first probe, for the death of the pretence that 'protected' heritage countryside is really protected, did not deflect the invasion.

How much is a view worth? How do you cost-account a landscape? Can a computer be programmed to evaluate bird song and the brief choreography of a young beech plantation against a May sky, a kestrel hovering in winter air? Is there a method of reckoning up the percentage in a person's inner replenishment from wild country?

No one bothers with these contemptible little sums, not when real money is involved. The seismographic team dynamited through the meadows and collected their data; the oil consortium's rig erectors swarmed in; they got all the permits they wanted from the men elected as the public's servants. Oil is profitable and vital to keep your car and my car running, so what's the fuss? What does it matter where it comes from and if steel towers are driven into Britain's remaining non-industrialized acres—even if we get less than one per cent of our needs from carving up our National Parks and scheduled Areas of Outstanding Natural Beauty into job-lots for mostly foreign investors, the scores of companies which are now X-raying all the kingdom for money-crops.

It is Whitehall policy. It is progress. It is modernization. It is growth. Or is it shrivelling what is most lastingly worthwhile?

I left the ledge and half-walked, half-jumped lower out of the slash of the wind, and out of eye range of the rig and its conurbation of metal cabins and trailers.

In the short term man seems to have it taped, to have

gained complete dominance over the planet; in the longer term I think we may be the losers. The temporary maiming and disfigurements will heal, and perhaps their scars will be a chart of what happened to the primitive barbarians who tried to milk the Earth dry and destroyed themselves by greed and arrogance.

*

On a sycamore's highest twig a strapping bird, marked like a leopard in front, is raking the dripping valley with loud screaking notes.

I hurry, log under arm, from the coppice. The air wraps around me like a wet bandage. The Knoll, the far ridge, the beech wood are all a faded sepia photograph, outlines almost erased. Uncheered by the mistle thrush's banshee song, I am anxious to get indoors, out of the short day already at its last gasp.

I enter the house where cacti droop in a fetid little conservatory. Living in my house has the feeling of being in a railway train shunted up a siding, for it is long and skinny with windows each side of the compartment-ish rooms.

At one end is what could pass for Stevenson's Rocket: all those curly black pipes, iron wheels and knobbly bolts of the slumbering turbines in the mill room. By passing from there through an interminable series of doors (down the length of unswaying carriages) you eventually reach the dining car.

Here the Aga throbs with heat. Dogs stretch nose to tail all the way under the ovens, melting the marrow of their backbones. One stage farther is the pantry, big as a guard's van, with wide cool slate shelves and whopping ceiling hooks where hams were hung.

The kitchen is where the gang hangs out. It is my favourite place. Earlier I was sidling down from my office overhead to wring out a third cup of tea and palm another steaming mince pie from the wire tray.

It is more than usually cluttered. The Welsh dresser is just normally piled like a rummage sale, with pliers, copies of *Mad*, pebbles from the beach, a paintbrush, the parish mag and some dried artichokes. Amid muddy gumboots the Windsor chair is invisible under duffle-coats and Afghan cloaks: a memorial mound to my twenty years of failure to get clothing hung up in cupboards.

The long elm table in the centre of the tiled floor is like a lost property counter. Unemptied shopping bags spill figs and paper parcels; unopened magazines are piled with boxes of moth-eaten decorations brought down from the attic yet again.

One son is eating what appears to be a large break-fast; the other has decided that a drink is due, and is sampling the rum which my wife is mixing into a sauce. Snatches of disjointed chat and urgent instructions occasionally beat the record player in volume. The butcher calls. The telephone rings. The kettle whistles. The dogs bark.

I have lost contact with reality. Beyond the glass door the garden wavers greyly and dream-like, and a robin perches on a tub, a small glowing bulb in the creeping twilight.

There is a sense of high vibrations mounting to the point where reason snaps and erratic behaviour may break out. My daughter, spraying tracer fire of purple cream from a metal gun, is writing on a cake's white icing: 'Merry Christmas To All Our Readers'.

I am beginning to suspect that something is afoot.

*

My children headed homeward from art school in the far north, from university two hundred miles east, from first job in the west. They converged upon this southerly base with a clatter of rusted wings and the throb of ruptured silencers.

How nice it is, in the turmoil of eleventh-hour shopping and furtive present-wrapping, to have them gathered together for Christmas. They will be able to deal with cutting the holly. I felt that my lily-white hands weren't up to such rough stuff.

I know where the scratchy sprigs can be got. I have had my eye on the tree. It stands in the wild hedge beside the stile at the foot of Round Knoll.

It is a fine mature forty-foot stalwart with a girth like a bull's—hollies grow big down here in the humid mildness. But until October I had not been sure if we could crop it for household decoration.

You can't tell with a holly. It may turn out to be the wrong sex. Some people are unreasonably resentful because, although their holly has creamy blooms in May, it doesn't generate a single spark of fruit.

They ask too much of it. They own a male whose business is dusting honey bees with yellow pollen, with which the flowers of a female tree—hopefully within whistling distance—can be fertilized.

We are lucky. Our holly is a plenteous she-tree. Its shellacked leaves glint in the pale, malt whisky wash of the winter sun. And its berries are brilliant as fairylights. It is a ready-made Christmas tree.

Apprehensively I had watched the chattering autumn flocks of fieldfares—strapping, gaudy thrushes from Scandinavia—looting along the hedgerows and gulping the berries like peanuts at a drinks party.

The clusters are so profuse that you can't see where their beaks dug in. There is enough for all.

So off through the frost-crackling mud my children and their friends went to bring back the bounty, and I made for the coppice to see about that trunk section I had ear-marked as being a likely looking Yule log when I had been picking up lighter stuff. Sloshing through pulpy leaves I came to it. Just what was needed. That would have roasting flames roaring up the chimney. But I was lacking one minor essential: a horse team and chains. Perhaps I should have dished out the tasks differently, seen to the holly myself and left the hauling of the log to all those restless young muscles.

I slunk back to the house and applied myself to the urgent labour of reading a review book at the fireside. It was considerate of me, I decided, to let the children get the holly. As they sorted it out in the crowded kitchen, plaiting a garland for the brass knocker and hanging it over the fire's cross-beam, they would be enacting fun and mystery as perennial as 'the rising of the sun and the running of the deer.'

Those words of *The Holly and the Ivy* were first recorded by folklorist Cecil Sharp in Gloucestershire; other versions were found in Somerset. It was sung in English villages long before it became a carol—perhaps long before Christ's birth, although holly leaves came to represent his crown of thorns. The word holly merged its meaning into holy, but anciently the tree was called 'holegn' and then the 'holm', which occurs in so many place names.

The original pagan symbolism was the entwining of the masculine holly with the feminine ivy, and the wreaths were hung where young men and girls danced at this pause when the sun is at its farthest point from the equator.

When the ice-armoured earth seemed dead, this was the sacrament to life continuing and rebirth in spring.

I heard the youthful voices returning across the field and looked out of the window. Across the lattice of bare branches in the afternoon's deepening iron light I saw our commonest evergreen shining scarlet, a lamp held up bright through the darkness of the winter solstice.

FRED ARCHER

UNDER THE PARISH LANTERN

The author writes:
'This was a land of cider, fat bacon and bread pudding. Of little master men who are gone. Gone too are the snaky bends in the lanes where the hawthorn hedges combed wisps of hay from loaded waggons. The straightened roads, wire fenced, stand stark and naked. Concrete kerbs have replaced roadside verges cut by the roadman's stock-axe, but it is still a good place to live. There is the smell of the new mown hay, the lambs gambol in apple blossomed orchards—and no street lamps, so we are still "Under the Parish Lantern".'
'It glows with the magical warmth of the age it re-creates'
Sir Bernard Miles

'Memories of rustic Worcestershire half a century ago, packed with the stuff and speech of village life and the tackle and tools of the farmer's round, illustrated with flesh and blood photographs of dogs and badgers, sprout-pickers and harvesters, that go with the text like pickled onions with cheese' *The Observer*

'An almost magical evocation of country life . . . in the lost England of the first World War and shortly after'
The Sunday Times

THE DISTANT SCENE

'goes a long way to restoring some of the right kind of robustness to the recent past' *The Countryman*

THE SECRETS OF BREDON HILL

'It acts on the computerised, pollution-scarred spirit of the seventies like a balm' *R. F. Delderfield*